This book is dedicated to my wife Jill and my incredible kids, Lucas, Kayla, Marcus, Jonas, Gabriel and Nicholas. Thank you for your support and patience as I pursue my dreams!

Copyright: 2017: The Business Funding Formula

1. What is the Business Funding Formula
2. $150 Million and Counting
3. Business Debt is Different than Personal Debt
4. Understanding Credit & Income
5. The Business Funding Formula
6. Do you have collateral?
7. Is SBA Possible for a Startup?
8. A Trick to Save you Thousands
9. Unsecured Term Loans
10. Traditional Lines of Credit
11. Revolving Credit Lines/Cards
12. Not ROI, but ROL
13. Humble, Not Entitled
14. Merchant Cash Advances - Be Careful
15. SBA For Established Businesses
16. Term Loans & Lines of Credit For Established Businesses (non SBA)
17. Business Credit & How it Works
18. Putting it All Together & Funding Followup
19. Full Service Funding vs Do It Yourself
20. IMPORTANT: Funding Rules to Live By

© The Business Funding Formula 2017

CHAPTER 1: WHAT IS THE BUSINESS FUNDING FORMULA?

Now that you've come across this book you're probably wondering what exactly is the business funding formula and how will it help me? If you're reading this, then you are either an entrepreneur or an aspiring entrepreneur, and you have realized that if you simply had access to capital and funding, you would have a real chance at building not only the business of your dreams, but the life of your dreams as well. The ability to secure capital can be the difference between success and failure in business: it is absolutely that important.

Before the recession of 2008 and 2009, it was not complicated to secure funding at your bank to launch or grow your business, but since then it has taken incredible creativity and knowledge to secure funding, especially for a new business with unproven financials. Even for businesses with history and financials, it is still difficult and even though several years have passed since the recession of 2008-09, banks and lenders still mostly lend to the top 5 to 10 percent of businesses and largely ignore the other 90 percent of small businesses who desperately need access to capital to have a chance to bring their products and services to market. To make matters worse, the proliferation of many different high-rate finance products and expensive lenders has made it even more confusing to find the best funding options to launch and grow your business.

The Business Funding Formula was created to give all business owners a step-by-step process to follow in order to secure the best funding possible to turn your entrepreneurial pursuits into the truth. The funding formula has existed for decades and has had a tremendous effect on some well known businesses that you recognize and probably use on a weekly or even daily basis. Without these business owners' understanding of the funding formula, it is very likely that their businesses would not exist any where near the level they do or may not even have survived without the funding formula.

The business funding formula is the holy grail for jump starting your new or existing business. You have probably seen some studies done by Ivy League schools and other organizations and noted that one of the top reasons new businesses fail is due to undercapitalization, a complicated term to describe running out of money. I don't care if you are selling lemonade on a table outside your house or a more complicated business model, it takes money to buy the cups, the lemonade, the table and the signs in the front yard to market your lemonade; so although it is popular to talk about starting a business, without any type of up-front money, it is simply for the most part not part of the capitalistic world we live in.

The business funding formula will break down the top funding options available for entrepreneurs including SBA, unsecured

© The Business Funding Formula 2017

loans, lines of credit, merchant cash advances, corporate credit, no income funding and every funding option available on the planet today. Most importantly, it will take all of this seemingly complicated BS and break it down into easily understandable steps to guide you to the best funding you can possibly qualify for. It will also provide you with hacks and tactics to save thousands on any financing you need for the rest of your life. This book will also pull back the curtain to how your credit score is calculated and how lenders make lending decisions. The business funding formula is a tool that every entrepreneur needs in order to achieve massive growth for a business.

The American Dream Is to Start Your Own Business
For many of the first settlers of America, the dream was to own your own property, work your own land and have your own home. With so many incredible technologies revolutionizing the way we live from Mark Zuckerberg's Facebook to Steve Job's Apple, there has been a new American Dream created: the dream of owning and running your own business.

As a business owner you have no limit to the amount of money you can make, and as the owner you set your own schedule. Life as an entrepreneur gives you the opportunity to create jobs and most importantly to create products and services that improve the way you live and can leave an indelible impact on humanity for years to come. Not to mention, that it is just plain cool being the person in charge, having the opportunity to earn everything you get, and as the owner the buck stops with you, there is no one to blame for your success or failure other than yourself. Without doubt it is easier to start a business in the United States than in most other countries around the world so if you reside in the US then very fortunate are you.

If you've ever spent time at an old folks' home or lost someone close to you that passed away too early, then you know our time here on this Earth is limited; we must live life to the fullest. Starting and running your own business is such a unique opportunity and one of the best ways I know of to grab life by the horns. Starting a business is the new American dream, and the ability to secure money to launch your business is a vital key to making that dream happen.

Capitalism Requires Capital

When entrepreneurs start a business, they typically begin by creating a product or service that solves a problem. That problem can be great or small, but rest assured there are several needs that each entrepreneur will need to satisfy in order to achieve success with a new business. Some of these needs are: money to pay your personal bills, capital for the development of your product or service, funding for an office space at some point, cash to pay your staff and financing for a marketing budget.

Suffice it to say if you do not have adequate capital to cover each or at least some of these initial expenses for your business, the odds of your business succeeding go down significantly. Money to cover your personal bills can be crucial; if you can't cover your personal bills it is very difficult to focus on growing your business.

Just as important is the ability to build a product or service that can generate sales and income immediately. If your business is predicated on some long term development of your product instead of generating income now, then you will need access to a lot of capital. Paying for a new website and social media pages as well as implementing marketing will all take a great deal of money. The bottom line is access to capital is a means to an end: it's not necessarily the capital that you care about, it's what it can do for you. It's how that money can help you to market your business, hire staff, get a nice office location, purchase inventory, build a top website and earn the opportunity to go full time with your business and quit your Damn job!

Venture Capital & Crowd Funding Fund 1 to 3% of Businesses: What about the other 97%?

Forbes has researched and studied venture capital and crowdfunding and while they are exciting funding solutions for some businesses, for the vast majority they are not really a possibility. Out of 100 business plans that VC firms look at, only one to two of them actually get venture capital funding. For the large number of new businesses that do not even approach a Venture Capital firm, the numbers drop below 1% of all businesses that actually receive VC money. Crowdfunding is not much different, while a larger number of entrepreneurs can receive some interest from crowdfunding, again the majority never reach their minimum funding needs.

The reason for the small percentage is that VC and crowdfunders are not looking for "normal" businesses, so unless you have the next facebook or iphone, your odds for securing VC or crowdfunding money are very small. Real estate, insurance, building, retail, restaurants, wholesale, cleaning, plumbing, electrical and most businesses are not in the wheelhouse for VC money. VC's want products or services like Uber that can have a tremendous impact and be sold to the entire population, again for most businesses that is not likely.

Crowdfunding is not much different. Unless you have a musical talent or a very unique product, then the odds of securing crowdfunding are very low. So that being reality, where do entrepreneurs go to find funding? Answer, the Business Funding Formula contains the funding solutions you need to launch your business.

Why Mark Cuban is Dead Wrong About Starting a business on a Loan

You may have seen Mark Cuban on the TV show *Shark Tank* or at least noticed that he is the owner of the NBA team the Dallas Mavericks. I am a big admirer of Mark Cuban and love the way he runs his businesses; however, he is dead wrong about some things. He has a youtube video with millions of views that states unequivocally that only an idiot would start a business on a loan. Why would Mark say that? Would it be because he would rather you go to Shark Tank so that he could give you 50k and take 50% of the ownership in your company? I know I would much rather keep half of my future profits which could be worth millions and simply secure 50k in funding without giving away any equity in my business. Check out these three stories that absolutely refute Mr. Cuban's position against securing a loan for your business.

The Richest Person In the World Knew the Funding Formula
If he were alive today, he would be the wealthiest person on the planet, and one of the driving forces behind his business was his knowledge of the business funding formula. Samuel Moore Walton started his first store in Newport, Arkansas, with a $20,000 loan plus a little money he had saved. In the first couple years he believed if he sold ice cream out in front of his store that he might be able to generate more store traffic. He had built credit and a relationship with a bank and was able to secure nearly $2,000 (a lot in the 1940's) and with that ice cream machine was able to not only generate more traffic, but also. more importantly. a healthy increase in sales volume from $80k to $225k within three years.
A few years later in 1962 when he opened the first Wal-Mart in Rogers, Arkansas, he did so with no venture capital, no investor money and certainly no crowdfunding. So how did he do it? He

© The Business Funding Formula 2017

had established strong business and personal credit with multiple banks, lenders and money contacts across the country. Thanks to his knowledge of the best funding options at the time, he was able to borrow "to the hilt," as he described in his book *Made in America*. In truth it is safe to say had Sam Walton not understood the funding formula, business credit and how lending works, the Wal-Mart we know and see all across the world would not exist today.

As of the date of this book, Wal-Mart is the top company in the world in terms of gross annual sales or revenues, generating nearly half a Trillion dollars in annual sales. Sam passed away in 1992 and left his shares to his children, but if he were still alive today based on the net worth of his children and family who still own his shares in Wal-Mart, he would be worth over $100 Billion today. He would be the richest person in the world. Understanding the business funding formula was crucial to the massive growth of Wal-mart.

How 40k in Credit Cards Built a Multi Billion Dollar Business

Perhaps you've seen the commercials for Under Armour, the innovative sports apparel business? The founder is Kevin Plank who had entrepreneurship flowing through his veins. In college at the university of Maryland, he started a rose business and sold a ton of flowers on Valentine's day, and he also sold t-shirts at concerts. From the profits of those businesses, he had about 20k saved up and he had smartly developed a strong credit history with 5 lenders who had each issued him credit cards.

© The Business Funding Formula 2017

Understanding that business debt is different from personal debt, he maxed out those 5 credit cards for a grand total of $40,000 in order to develop his innovative product and market it. A year later he was broke, but he persevered and landed his first sale to Georgia Tech for about 17k. Next, 2 dozen NFL teams purchased his product, and now we see commercials with Steph Curry of the Golden State Warriors and many other athletes who promote the company. The company now does nearly $2 Billion in sales and has over 5,900 employees, and Kevin Plank who had started the company on 5 credit cards is now a Billionaire. Had he not known how to develop credit and secure several larger limit credit cards, Under Armour may not exist today. The ability to follow the funding formula and secure funding was vital to Under Armour's launch.

How a Bankrupt internet icon built an 8 figure business with Credit Partners

Brendon Burchard is an internet superstar and a best selling author of several books. He speaks on stages across the country with former Presidents of the United States and even Oprah trusts him to create her online products. Before he became an internet icon with over 50 million views on Youtube, he was a bankrupt entrepreneur. A significant amount of people were unable to stay solvent through the great recession, and bankruptcy became their only way to move forward. So what do you do when your credit is smashed, and no lender will give you more than $500? As Brendon faced this dilemma, he could have become negative, given up on his dreams and let fear destroy him. Instead he found a funding solution by connecting with family and friends who had great credit and confidence in his business.

In one of his first major events he rented a circus tent in order to fill it full of excited followers of his life changing strategies. The city immediately began to issue him tickets for not having big enough generators and other infrastructure up to code. Fortunately before that, he had already followed the funding formula and established revolving credit lines with his family and friends, who then allowed him to utilize those revolving credit lines to cover costs.

Fast forward a few years later and Brendon now has a following of millions, and his business generates over 8 figures in annual sales and is growing. Without access to capital at the beginning of his business, he likely would have failed, so if it is not becoming clear to you by now, this is how important funding is for your business to have a chance to succeed. Of course just having access to funding does not guarantee success, but with it, the odds are certainly more in your favor!

Master Funding and You Have a Chance to Build the Business of Your Dreams

© The Business Funding Formula 2017

It doesn't matter what kind of business you are building, there are two certainties I have seen play over time and again when an entrepreneur starts a new business. I have seen these two challenges every time I have launched my own businesses or helped my clients who are beginning their new ventures. The first is for some reason your initial cost estimates to start your business always seem to end up costing more than you had anticipated. There may be extra deposits to the manufacturer of your product or to secure your office space. There might be additional taxes and fees in order to establish payroll and pay your employees: it just seems to happen that way. So if you haven't secured as much capital as possible prior to launching your business, you will face tremendous cost hurdles to jump over.

The second challenge that inevitably seems to confront most entrepreneurs is that it takes longer to begin generating sales and revenue. Your pretty pro forma might have shown you jumping from 10k in monthly sales to 50k in monthly sales within 6 months and for some reason it ends up taking you 12 months to get to those numbers. I believe that starting a business endeavor is the most rewarding, exciting way to build a career that you love, but buyer beware it will require a long-term vision and patience. The ability to secure capital and affordable funding will be vital in order to persist and endure until you create the business of your dreams.

To find out how much funding you can qualify for, go to www.LeoKanell.com and we will tell you within 24 hours what your Custom Funding Plan might look like for free.

© The Business Funding Formula 2017

CHAPTER 2: $150 MILLION & COUNTING

Over a Decade of Funding

Now that we have established why business funding is so vital and how the funding formula will help you to jump start your business, I want to tell you why I know funding. For the past 15 years I have been involved in many areas of funding and lending. I have been fortunate to help to secure funding for thousands of clients for many purposes such as startup funding, equipment financing, sba loans, commercial real estate, residential real estate, inventory funding, short term funding and longer term financing. My teams and I have helped to secure over $150 Million dollars in funding, and that number is growing each and every month.

Whether you are looking for lines of credit, term loans, revolving credit lines, secured loans and any type of funding, the underwriting guidelines are all similar. I have made it my life mission to keep my finger on the pulse of the business funding sector. The so-called C's of funding are credit, collateral, capacity to repay and other auxiliary factors like how you manage your cash flow. Every day, month and year my team and I secure funding for our clients who are new and established business owners all across the country.

In the past few years the internet has brought about a lot of new lending groups both private and public and there are a lot of different options, but mostly there is significant confusion regarding what funding is best. What I have found in dealing with thousands of clients is that most people just want someone who is an expert in funding to guide them to the very best funding that they would get for themselves.

The business funding formula and this book will break down the very best funding options and the formula to follow to secure the best funding.

Funding My Own Businesses
I have always been a believer in being a product of your product, so if I help entrepreneurs to secure funding then I need to be walking the walk and doing the same to fund my business ventures. Not only have I used parts of the funding formula to fund a business, but I have actually done it several times with different businesses.

5k To Start a House Painting Business
Since the age of 21 I have been self-employed and owned various businesses. Along the way I have had some fun and challenging journeys to secure money for each business. The key to these true, personal stories of how I secured money for my businesses is that there is no one-size-fits-all package; the point is that there are many unique ways to secure financing, and the key is creativity, so let's get to it.

My first business was a house painting business, I knew nothing about painting, and I was extremely broke, newly married and driving a 15 year old beat up Toyota Corolla with 250k miles on it. I needed money for equipment like a paint sprayer, ladders, tape, paper, plastic and enough to buy paint for our first jobs before we would get paid. I needed about $5,000. My mentor had a solution for me, so he simply negotiated a $5,000 line of credit at the local paint store, I was able to get the ladders, paint brushes, rollers, sprayer, everything I needed to get the business going even though I had no credit and no money.

From that day on I learned that if you want to build a business badly enough, there is always a way to do so: it just takes a little creativity. To be an entrepreneur is to be creative, focused and obsessed about your business, and you will find a financing solution. Best of all, out of 100 competitors in my state I finished 2nd and ran a $60,000 business that summer and made enough to pay for my honeymoon with my wife to Cancun, Mexico!

In this example, the key to financing my business was working out a credit line with a local paint store supplier, so if your business is dependent on vendors like this, workout short-term financing options, and that may be a huge breakthrough for your business.

40k to start a Home Loan Brokerage

Fast forward 3 years later, and an associate of mine and I were looking to start a home loan brokerage. We had ambitious plans: we would hire 20 loan officers, get a nice office, fill it full of computers and furniture and make a fortune. Just one problem, we didn't have a lot of money, no collateral, and no business financials as proof that we were a proven business with low risk for a bank to lend to. What were we to do?

About a year before I had just bought my 2nd house at the age of 24. I thought I was pretty cool; I bought it from a bank foreclosure sale for 250k, 4k sq ft, on a hill, 7 beds, 4 baths, and my family helped us gut it. This thing was a mess: there was literally dog crap and pee stuck to the carpets and so forth. Apparently there had been some crazy Russian mafia guy who owned it and swat had at one point had to break down the door to take out his gang. Back to the money problem

© The Business Funding Formula 2017

at hand. I had some money, but not a lot to fix it up. By this time I had established some credit, I had bought a house with a mortgage at the age of 23, and I had bought my first new car. So I had started to learn how to utilize credit to make things happen.

So of course we worked out a credit line for carpet, paint, countertops, kitchen appliances, and after securing at least 30k in credit at some local stores, we were able to get the house fixed up just like new. So back to my original problem at hand. I needed 40k to begin my new business, and I realized that since we had bought the house at a low price and put in some sweat equity that indeed we had some equity available. Home equity can provide funding solutions for your business. So I found a company that was willing to finance a home equity line of credit; the only problem was that they had to use all of the money to pay off all of the store credit lines used for the carpet, countertops and paint. Even our two car loans had to be paid off in order to qualify for the loan, so I went ahead and did it. Just one problem: there wasn't a cent left to finance my new business.

After brainstorming I realized, hey, I now have my two cars worth about 40k owned free and clear, so I strolled into my local credit union where I banked and went ahead and secured two auto loans for a total of $40,000 cash. And then I had a little celebration because, yes, it is such a sweet feeling to secure the money needed to move your dreams forward. By the end of our full first year in business, we had revenues of nearly $2,000,000 all from that 40k in funding.

The Key lesson in this example is to utilize lazy assets that you have equity in that aren't making money and use those to secure money for your business. The two most common are auto loans and home equity lines of credit, but if you own any asset that has a title to it, you can often find cash financing for any car, boat, trailer, rv, motorcycle or vehicle that you own. Home equity lines of credit are especially a wonderfully cheap alternative to finance your new or existing business. Another asset you can tap is a 401k or IRA from an old job. You can often get loans from those and finance your business that way as well.

300k in order to refurbish a property and sell it for $2M (not counting the mortgage)

About a year later our home loan company was doing pretty well, and this was at the height of the real estate boom, so, of course, we wanted to go big in that market (maybe not such a great idea, but we did it anyway.) My wife was driving through a neighborhood close to our home and noticed a 9k sq ft mansion on a 2 acre estate right on a private golf course. The property was a little older but was selling for way under value at 1.3M.

Back before the real estate mess, of course financing for a mortgage secured by a house wasn't impossible to get, and we were cash flowing pretty good at our business, so we were able to qualify for financing. We closed on the house and were ready to go to work. One problem: we needed about 300k cash to fix up the house. We had about 50k to 60k saved up, nowhere near close to the 300k that we would need to be able to sell the house at top price. We did have a couple of corporations, LLC's that we had built up some business credit for, so my partner and I went to see not one, but about 8 to 10 banks and credit unions.

© The Business Funding Formula 2017

Before we went in to these financial institutions we made sure we had a solid foundation with basic items, for example we had a business location for our office, and we had a dedicated business phone number. Our email wasn't a gmail or personal email but was the name of our business.com. The secretary of state website had us each listed as an owner/member of the business. These little items make a huge difference when it comes to securing money for a business. We asked about their financing products, all of them, and instead of asking for one loan for $300,000 (which is a huge mistake that most people make) we asked for lower, smaller amounts, and we were able to secure anywhere from $10,000 to $45,000 at each bank/credit union.

When it was all said and done, we were able to just barely secure about $300,000 in combined credit lines with our small savings. We found a great contractor to spearhead the entire project, and about a year later we were finally ready to list the property. It sold for $2M, and we netted nearly 350k on that deal: thanks to the financing we were able to secure creatively.

Bottom line lesson as Tony Robbins often says, "When you say that you don't have the money to make your business dreams happen, that is just not true." If you are creative and obsessed enough, there are financing solutions. This particular financing solution's keys are tied to the importance of building a corporation with good credit as well as making sure the foundation of the business is solid. Simple items like having a company website, email, business/commercial address, business license, being registered properly with the secretary of state for corporations in your state all build credibility. Of course solid personal credit plays a big part in the equation to successful funding. In the next story I will show you how to secure money even when you don't have good credit.

How I Secured 365k in Cash Credit Lines and Loans with Horrible Credit

Fast forward a few years later to the middle of the great recession. We had made some profits which we had reinvested in other real estate that we then failed to sell. The net result was that we no longer had good personal or business credit any more: a predicament that many people found themselves stuck with. So at this point we had several ideas for some businesses that had proven profitable on a smaller scale, and now it was time to go ahead and scale it up. But you guessed it, we needed a lot more money than we currently had. In order to get those businesses off the ground and grow them, we needed funding; and this time we didn't have the credit to qualify, so we were kind of just stuck.

Day after day passed and week after week went by and our little business was making money each day; but at its current pace, we would never truly grow it. We would never build it to where it would truly reap sufficient profits to make the long hours worth it. We were truly frustrated and began to search for solutions.

Business credit:
We started to hear about this magical thing called business credit, where you could build a strong business credit score with the main business credit bureaus and secure funding without needing good

personal credit. We learned about Dun & Bradstreet (the biggest business credit bureau) we learned about business experian, we also learned about equifax business credit. So for $2500 we purchased a package from a company in Nevada. We set up a Nevada corporation and began the task of building corporate credit. The only way to build up personal and business credit is to, of course, buy things on credit and then make timely payments. So we began buying office supplies like paper, printer ink, cleaning supplies and everything that was fairly affordable in an effort to build what we thought would be our pathway to money.

Several weeks passed; we began to build up our business credit and obtain some positive business credit history. I remember we had to buy weird things like big, heavy work boots and clothes. We got some mouse pads, keyboard cleaner, and then we got a net 30 gas card to get gas for business purposes. Fast forward a few weeks later, and we now had pretty good credit on our business, and then we got to thinking, what if we did this with multiple business entities? So next we went ahead and set up some new business entities and began the process of building the credit with those corporations. We finally progressed to where we were able to get some sizeable credit lines with Amazon, Staples and Chevron. Everything was looking good; we had secured financing based solely on our business tax id alone without ever listing our ssn on our applications: this was really cool. Then we ran into a little problem. It was nice to have credit at Staples to buy things and also at Amazon, but in reality we were hoping for 50k to 100k in cash credit lines that we could use how we wanted. Before the recession, this might have been possible, but with credit tightened and banks being heavily regulated, (with little change even up until this day) I realized that corporate credit would likely only get us so far. In

© The Business Funding Formula 2017

order to secure lots of usable cash type credit lines with the freedom to spend the money how I wanted to, I was going to need to have good credit. So we had spent close to $5,000 or more at this point and were really not in a better position to secure cash usable credit lines than when we first began the process. So there we were frustrated and still stuck, now what….

Then it hit me, ok if the only way I'm going to get money to grow our businesses was with good personal credit, I realized the solution was simple. Now this solution may sound simple, but it really is a tremendous breakthrough for entrepreneurs who have a proven business model and are confident and passionate with their business but have poor personal credit. This is how they can get financing even with bad personal credit.

Each business owner who is truly sold on his or her business will probably have no issue going to ask friends and family for money to grow their business, but unless you have a really rich uncle who loves you, that is usually a pretty tall task. However, if you ask them to co-sign for funding for your business, and you recruit them to your business and give them some sort of compensation/equity for co-signing for funding for your business, then you have a real chance.

We all know at least one person in our family or circle of friends who has good credit and would be willing to help co-sign for some funding to grow your business. Anyone truly serious about their business will find that one credit partner and bring them aboard. This is much easier than trying to convince someone to loan you hard earned money.

WORD OF WARNING: You must explain honestly that there are risks for any business, and so there are of course risks to your credit partner
© The Business Funding Formula 2017

including of course their good credit score. Tell your credit partner the truth and make sure they are legally covered with a contract for compensation, shares in the company, profit sharing or some fair form of compensation.

So immediately we put together a full business plan, some projections of how our business could grow, and we made a deal with a couple of family members and a few friends, each had decent credit scores above 680, so we used a similar plan that we had successfully used a few years ago and submitted funding applications for some credit lines and loans for each of the business entities that we had built business credit with. Each partner legally came aboard as a partner of each business and a real stake in the future profits of each business. The results were excellent. When it was all said and done, we had secured about $350,000 with the help of 6 partners who had excellent credit: not too shabby.

The bottom line lesson from the funding that we finally secured was building business credit can help you to secure money for your business, but typically only small credit lines limited to the stores that issue them. The process is also slow and costly. It really only helps if you have good personal credit or a credit partner to join the business that has good credit, good corporate credit isn't enough to secure cash credit lines that you can use how you want. The moral of the story in this case was don't waste thousands chasing a white elephant when the solution is simple: find one person, (it only takes one) who will join your business that has good personal credit and together you will be able to secure the money you need for your business.

© The Business Funding Formula 2017

This principle also applies to those entrepreneurs with bad credit who think that if they pay thousands and spend months with a credit repair company they will then be ready for funding. In reality if all of the negative items are removed from your credit, but there are no active positive major accounts like a mortgage, car loan and decent sized credit card, then all of your time, money and resources would be better spent on finding a credit partner to join your business and co-sign for it.

An important rule to follow with funding secured by credit lines/credit cards is to only use half of the funding and leave the other half in there for emergencies including making monthly payments in case it takes longer to generate sales and profits than you planned on.

I am Passionate About Funding

My mission is to help entrepreneurs to secure the most affordable growth capital in order to jump start their business ventures and turn their dreams into the truth! Nothing brings a smile to my face like seeing one of my clients secure affordable funding and have a chance to live their dream of being a business owner and creating products and services that drive our local economies and bring value to others. In truth without the ability to access funding many businesses either never take off or are simply mired in mediocrity. I truly believe it has never been more confusing to secure funding than it is today, so join me on this journey as I present the business funding formula as a great tool to jumpstart your business. I am the CEO and Founder of Leo Kanell (Funding) and, of course, the author and creator of the Business Funding Formula.

To find out how much funding you can qualify for, go to www.LeoKanell.com and we will tell you within 24 hours what your Custom Funding Plan might look like for free.

© The Business Funding Formula 2017

CHAPTER 3: BUSINESS DEBT IS DIFFERENT THAN PERSONAL DEBT

Personal Debt Can Enslave

Debt has a lot of negative connotations to it, and with so-called experts like Dave Ramsey and Suze Orman constantly telling us how bad debt is, it's no wonder the word brings nausea to most of us. Naturally when you think about securing funding on a loan or line of credit, there can be some trepidation or hesitance to move forward with funding. However, business debt is significantly different from personal debt, but before we analyze the differences, let's take a look at personal debt.

Personal debt can take many forms including personal mortgages, car loans, credit cards and the dreaded student loan. It can be argued that some types of personal debt make us money, but for the most part when we buy expensive cars, houses, clothes and vacations on credit cards or even 6 figure student loans that may not actually make us more money in the long run we are legitimately being harnessed with modern slavery. There is little doubt that excessive debt can enslave us and make it difficult to save money for investments.

You've probably heard the term house poor, where you purchase an overly expensive house and have no money left over in order to even go to a movie or buy your child a birthday gift. The reality is that I have seen tens of thousands of credit reports and probably 40 percent of the population has excessive debt obligations that make it nearly impossible for them to get ahead. Often I see aspiring entrepreneurs that have literally 50k to 100k in maxed out credit cards as well as overly expensive car loans and mortgages. The funny thing is that people can be just as broke making $150k per year as they can making $50k per year. Controlling personal expenses is helpful because overloaded personal debt can take over your life.

Personal Debt Generally Does Not Make You Money

A wise man once said the only acceptable kind of debt is a reasonable mortgage and maybe one car loan, but other than that personal debt does not make much sense. That same man represented one of the more financially conservative churches in the US, so when I saw that his organization had a brochure on how to start a business and actually indicated that business debt was ok versus the need to avoid personal debt, it really struck me how true his words were. I think one of the reasons for that belief is that personal debt rarely makes us money. Sure we need a car to get to work, but do we need that 45k new bmw or would a 2 year old buick for 23k make more sense? Many people mistakenly think that a house is a great investment: the reality is that in the first 10 years very little of your mortgage payment goes to your principal and by the time you add in closing costs, realtor commissions and the pit of money it takes to upkeep a house, you begin to realize maybe a house is not such a great investment and doesn't usually generate money in the short term.

Utilizing your credit cards to go on vacation, buy expensive furnishings for your residence and other numerous purchases just simply take our money each month without generating any income streams to actually pay for them and by the time you add in the compounding interest, you have truly compounded your financial burden. It can be argued that student loans will eventually make the borrower money; however, unless you are becoming a doctor, lawyer or engineer where a degree is necessary and will make you money, then student loans may not make you money. Many college grads go into fields or entry level positions where their college degree provided no purpose or return. So if you go blindly to college and fund your studies with student loans, then, again, it may not make you much money personally.

Why Business Debt is Different
Business debt is different from personal debt because it can and should make you money. In fact, it should generate income to more

than cover the cost of paying back the money and leave you a profit. Personal income rarely generates income to pay for itself, yet we often take on personal debt for a number of unjustified reasons. Yet when we consider securing funding for a business that can actually make us money, we hesitate to make the more logical decision of securing business funding. Now, realize that not all business debt makes sense: you need to secure funding that works for your business type and for the purpose that you need the funding for. In order to illustrate the point in a nice easy to follow format, let's' take a look at some examples of how business debt can make you money.

Business Financed Inventory

Let's say that you are selling furniture and can buy it wholesale at $200 per couch and then turn around and sell that couch in your retail store for $800 per couch. You decide to buy 50 couches for a total cost of $10,000. Let's say that you secure a $10,000 loan at a terrible 25% interest rate to be paid back over the next 12 months. Would it make sense to take a loan out at such a high rate and quick pay back? Ask one of the so-called financial gurus, and they may say no. It's just too expensive, but they would be completely wrong; let's do the math.

- $10,000 Loan
- $2,500 Interest (25%)
- Total Pay Back $12,500 over 12 months

Remember though that you are selling each couch at $800, but then the competition drops the price and you have to adjust and sell at $600 per couch, now let's look at your income

- $600 per couch x 50 couches sold over 12 months = $30,000
- $30,000 in income
- -$12,500 in loan and interest
- = $17,500 net Income

© The Business Funding Formula 2017

Now imagine that you had not taken out that loan. You would not have had the additional inventory, you would not have had the additional sales and you would not have made the additional $17,500 in profit.

Business Financed Marketing

Let's look at another example. Imagine you are going to invest in an online marketing campaign on Facebook. Let's say that you run an auto body shop and that your average body fixup is $1,000. You know from your research and testing that for every $500 in facebook advertising that you should generate two new auto body fixups. This time, let's use more expensive funding terms from the previous example, $10,000 @ 30%

- $10,000 Loan
- $3,000 Interest (30%)
- Total Pay Back $13,000 over 12 months

So if you spend $10,000 and generate 2 new auto body fixups @ $1k per job on average, how does it break down?

- $1,000 per job x 2 jobs per $500 spent on facebook = $2,000 per $500 spent on marketing.
- Spend $10,000/$500 = 20 x $2,000 (2 jobs per $500 spent on ads)
- = $40,000 in Total Income/Revenues
- -$13,000 in loan and interest
- $27,000 in Net Income

Now imagine that you had not taken out that loan. You would not have had the additional inventory, you would not have had the additional sales and you would not have made the additional $27,000 in profit. And that was at a pretty high rate and quick pay back.

Business Debt Can Make You Money
© The Business Funding Formula 2017

The two previous examples show clearly how business debt at even below average terms can still be incredibly beneficial to your business. One of the biggest points to realize is that in the previous examples the business owner literally would not have made that additional income and profit without taking out what most people would consider a very expensive loan. It requires some simple math, but it's not rocket science. Whenever you are about to secure funding, these are the types of scenarios you should break down. Then even if your numbers end up changing slightly to your detriment, you are still coming out on top and generating new income and profits that you would not have made without the funding.

To find out how much funding you can qualify for, go to www.LeoKanell.com and we will tell you within 24 hours what your Custom Funding Plan might look like for free.

© The Business Funding Formula 2017

Chapter 4: Understanding Credit & Income

Personal Credit is Vital for 99% of Business Owners (Biz Credit in chap 17)

Whether you are an aspiring entrepreneur or a veteran, your personal credit profile will always play an important role in your ability to secure funding and grow your business. In this chapter I want to share everything that I have learned in reviewing and assessing tens of thousands of credit reports. There are some simple things that you can do to increase your credit score and strengthen your credit profile. It is essential to understand as an entrepreneur that it is your job to educate yourself on how best to build your personal credit profile as that will open the door to more opportunities to grow your business.

The first step is to understand how your credit score is calculated and then how best to monitor your credit. Next, understanding the differences between installment and revolving accounts as well as the importance of avoiding public records and managing inquiries are all important factors to understanding your credit profile. Later on we will delve into how lenders look at your personal income and how that plays a role in funding both personally and also from a business funding standpoint.

© The Business Funding Formula 2017

What if My Credit Sucks?

Work on rebuilding your credit at www.LeoKanell.com, we have free credit enhancement tips and the most affordable credit repair service that I have seen on the market.

Credit Education is Increasing

Another way the internet has made our lives better is the opportunity to learn more about how to properly manage our credit profiles. There are 3 personal credit bureaus that give us credit scores, profiles and account reports: Experian, Equifax and Transunion. All 3 are important and necessary to maintain in order to have a strong credit profile. More lenders tend to use Experian, although there has been additional marketing the last few years that has increased the usage by lenders of equifax and transunion. Let's take a look at how credit scores are calculated.

How is Your Credit Score Calculated?

Credit scores range from 350 to 850 and are generated by all 3 credit bureaus (Experian, Equifax and Transunion) using the FICO method, which stands for Fair Isaac Corporation. Fair Isaac Corp was formed in California by some mathematicians who invented a risk model so that lenders could make good lending decisions. Credit scores above a 760 are top tier for most lenders, a 720 is still considered excellent credit, and a 680 is good solid credit. A 650 is average and the very lowest that most lenders will go for any decent type of funding.

35 percent of your credit score is based on your ability to make your payments on time.

That said on time is defined as being paid within 29 days of the due date. A negative mark on your credit will only happen officially when you are 30 days past due, so if you have been 5, 10 or even 29 days past due, there should be no adverse effects to your score or late payment reported. The more recent any late payments are reported, the more impact it will have on your credit score. So with business funding it is damn important to make your payments on time in the last year or two before applying for funding. If you had late payments 3 or 4 years ago and they were 30 to 59 days late, then the impact should not affect you as much as any late payments in the last 6 to 12 months will.

30 percent of your score is based on credit utilization.
This means that if you have several new auto loans that have balances close to the original loan amount, then your score will be affected. If you have 4 or 5 credit card accounts maxed out and the majority of your limits are used up, then that will cause your credit score to take a dip as well. If you use less than 50 percent or even less than 25 percent of your limits, then your score will generally be high.

15 percent of your score is based on how old your credit profile is.
The longer your accounts have been open, the stronger your credit will be. This is why it is usually very difficult for borrowers in their young 20's to have higher credit scores because they usually have limited credit histories with much less credit established as well as average age of accounts that only have a few months of history. Someone who is 60 years old may have 40 years of credit history, so for older borrowers the scoring model often will reward them for having accounts that may be decades old and show lenders that they are a good bet to lend to.

10 percent of your score is dependent on new credit & hard inquiries.

If you open several new accounts like multiple car loans, credit cards and student loans, in the short term it will hurt your score. Hard credit inquiries will also have a negative impact on your credit score; however, if your credit profile is strong with multiple established accounts and years of solid history, then the effects of credit inquiries will be more minimal. If you have a younger, newer credit profile, the newer hard credit inquiries will have a more profound effect on your score. One thing I have seen in thousands of business owners we have helped with funding is that they are aware of the negative impact that inquiries have on credit, and, in fact, actually have been led to believe that hard inquiries will absolutely ruin their life and credit score. Clearly this is not the case as credit inquiries only make up 10 percent or less of your score. That said acting strategically with credit inquiries is important.

10% of your score is connected to having multiple credit account types.

So if you have a good mix of installment loans like auto loans, revolving accounts like credit cards and mortgage real estate loans, then this section of your credit score will be marked high. So that is how our personal credit scores are calculated. Now you know, and knowing is half the battle! It is good to have a nice mix of different account types.

Credit Monitoring Organizations Are Not Created Equal

There are a number of credit monitoring organizations that have popped up in the last few years. There is, of course, credit monitoring directly at Experian.com, Equifax.com and transunion.com. There is also Myfico.com, CreditKarma.com, ScoreSense.com and CreditCheckTotal.com. Again having looked at tens of thousands of credit reports including reports from each of the aforementioned sites, I can tell you with absolute certainty that the most accurate credit report and score that is available on the market today is found at either www.ScoreSense.com or www.CreditCheckTotal.com, which is powered by Experian. The scores are extremely accurate, and the reporting is the most accurate as well.

I have seen credit reports from Credit Karma showing a 750 score, but when compared with CreditCheckTotal or ScoreSense, the more accurate score of 650 is displayed. Since credit does play such an important role, I definitely recommend paying the $29.95 each month in order to monitor your credit score and report for accuracy. One trick is to call them up and threaten to cancel, and they will generally drop your monthly fee down to $10 or $15.

Mortgage & Installment Accounts

Installment accounts are any type of credit account on our credit report that has a fixed term and fixed monthly payment to pay back the loan received. Examples of installment loans are mortgages, car loans, unsecured term loans, student loans, second mortgages, motorcycle loans, boat loans and typically any loan secured with collateral and paid back in a specific number of months. Generally speaking secured loans are easier to qualify for than unsecured installment loans. The reason being that if you do not make payment on your secured loan, the lender can simply take back the collateral like a car, property or any tangible asset used to secure the loan. Unsecured term loans have no security, no collateral and obviously represent a higher risk to the lender which is why unsecured term loans usually have higher rates than secured loans in order to compensate for the higher risk the lender takes. If you fail to repay the unsecured loan, then the lender is just out of luck. It is obviously helpful to your credit to have multiple installment accounts with several years of history.

Revolving Credit Accounts (Credit Cards) (Important trick about these accounts in Chapter 8)
So revolving credit accounts on your credit report are typically in three categories: credit cards, lines of credit and home equity lines of credit (secured). The most seen revolving account that shows on most credit reports are credit cards. These can be the more flexible use, well known types like American Express and Capital One or it can be small store accounts at your local clothing store at the mall that offers small revolving credit card accounts through Synchrony bank.

Lines of credit are more rare and typically issued by local banks and credit unions where borrowers have established extensive credit history to merit a larger, more traditional line of credit with easier cash access than a typical credit card. Home equity lines of credit may sometimes fall into a separate category of real estate, but they are most certainly secured revolving accounts and in terms of rates and terms generally have the lowest, best interest rates. Establishing multiple revolving credit lines including larger limit revolving accounts will generally increase your credit score and strengthen your credit profile.

Credit Inquiries (Will they ruin your life?)
I would say one of the most misunderstood parts of credit is credit inquiries. Credit inquiries are classified in two way: soft and hard

© The Business Funding Formula 2017

inquiries. Soft inquiries have no effect on your credit and are pulled by lenders who have given you credit already for the most part. They typically soft pull an updated report most months. For example, if your local credit union has given you a $5,000 credit card they will soft pull your credit each month to see if anything negative is on the horizon like late payments or heavy credit utilization. If they believe you are about to come into hard times they may cut your credit limit.

Some unsecured term lenders have also begun to do soft pulls for initial pre-approvals, so borrowers can find out what they qualify for without taking a hard inquiry. Hard inquiries can have a negative impact on your credit score and profile, but as we discussed previously, inquiries make up 10 percent or less of your actual credit score. The stronger and more established your credit the lesser the impact, the thinner and newer your credit profile is, the bigger impact a few credit inquiries will have on your credit. In most cases credit inquiries are not typically deal killers with secured loans like home loans and car loans; however, with unsecured funding like credit cards, credit inquiries can be a big deal. Common sense will take you far with credit inquiries: only take credit inquiries when you are committed to moving forward with some type of financing. At the same time it is essential to accept and understand that a few credit inquiries will not ruin your credit score or life and in most cases it is impossible to secure funding without taking some hard inquiries.

Public Records are Killers
Public records on your credit report come in the form of bankruptcies, judgments and tax liens. Each has a tremendously negative effect on your credit report and score. The older a bankruptcy the lesser effect it has on financing, but the fact of still having it listed on your report will

always be a negative factor with any financing you request. Judgments and tax liens often come down to the size of each judgment or tax lien. Those that fall under $1,000 typically don't have as big a downside as those that are several thousands of dollars. Often a judgment or tax lien will continue to report to your credit even after it is paid and released which is why it is imperative to avoid these negative public records at any cost.

Understanding Your Personal Income (Biz Income in chap 15 & 16)

For many business lenders the business owner's personal income plays a role in extending credit to you as a business owner. I've heard a lot of business owners ask me why and point out that the business is separate from their personal, but in reality lenders never see it that way. If your business struggles to bring in sales then it stands to reason that you will have a tough time paying your personal bills. So if you have extensive personal debt and bills then your business will need to produce enough profits for you to be able to pay your personal debts and have enough leftover to cover the cost of any new business loan or credit line.

Personal income typically breaks down into 2 types: employee/w2 income & self employed income. If you have employee, w2 wages then your employer has your taxes taken out of your paycheck and sends you the rest as well as a W-2 form at the beginning of each year for your previous year's work. If you are self employed then you may pay yourself a W-2, receive 1099 income and in most cases will have income from your business paid out from your business in the form of a k-1 or through your schedule C on your personal tax return.

© The Business Funding Formula 2017

Lenders Love W2 for Stability & Predictability

For unsecured term loans and traditional lines of credit secured personally, lenders love to see W-2 wage income. They have extensive data that shows that more often people with W-2 income are able to pay back at a more consistent rate than self employed borrowers. The other factor is W-2 income is extremely easy to calculate for a lender to know how much is available to service new debt or loan payments. So if you are still employed and looking for funding, keep that job until you secure funding and your business starts to gain traction.

Self Employment Income

Conversely, lenders do not love self employed borrowers for personal term loans, lines of credit and credit cards again because their data shows self employed borrowers have more volatile income and also because it is much more difficult to calculate. While a W-2 borrower can produce a W-2 and pay stub to qualify for different funding, a self employed borrower must produce all pages of the last 2 years of personal tax returns on the federal form 1040. The magic line that lenders use to calculate the income that a self employed borrower earns is located on line 37 which is at the bottom of page 1 of the personal tax return on form 1040. This line will include all 1099 income, business income, wages, capital gains and all income types and is what lenders use in calculating your income for a mortgage, car loan or unsecured term loan or line of credit.

Put it all Together

When it comes to business funding, personal funding and any kind of financing it is vital that you understand how credit works, how credit scores are calculated and how lenders will look at your income. The

© The Business Funding Formula 2017

more you can work on building your personal income and strengthening your personal credit profile, the more funding options you will have for your business and for any financing in general. Again the belief I carry and believe wholeheartedly to be true is that business debt is good debt that generates money for you and personal debt is generally not good as it just takes your money each month.

Debt that is paid for by others is good debt. Look at a rental property that you own that has a mortgage on it, that mortgage payment is paid by your tenant each month, the interest is a tax write off, the property depreciation is a tax write off, so this is a good example of good business debt. That huge $8k monthly mortgage payment and 1k mercedes benz payment are really not making you money and neither is that maxed out 15k credit card full of wasteful purchases from expensive retail stores and other non money making opportunities. Just learning the details about credit and income will help you for the rest of your life and be key to your business funding success.

To find out how much funding you can qualify for, go to www.LeoKanell.com and we will tell you within 24 hours what your Custom Funding Plan might look like for free.

Chapter 5: The Business Funding Formula

How to Use the Business Funding Formula

The best way to use the business funding formula is to simply follow the steps as broken down and explained in this chapter. The formula will lead you to the best funding you can qualify for without wasting time wondering if there is some magical funding option available that you are not aware of. Additionally, the business funding formula will open you up to funding combinations as well as actually prepare you to be able to qualify for funding.

In simpler terms without the funding formula, you go waste your time applying and getting denied when had you but known a few little steps you could have taken to qualify beforehand, you'd have saved yourself a lot of time and more importantly actually gotten approved. The biggest problem with just shooting in the dark and hoping for the best funding is that you often will not qualify, but with the funding formula and the answers to the funding test found here you will know exactly what you need to do in order to qualify for funding to launch your business to the next level. Follow these steps and then dig into each to find your funding solutions.

STEP 1: Are you a Startup or Established Business

The first thing that you will want to do is to determine if your business is classified as a startup or established business. There are 2 key points to look at:
1. Time in business
2. Annual Sales or Revenue

Time in Business
Regarding time in business if your business is less than 2 and to be even more accurate probably if it is less than 3 years old then your business will most likely fall into the startup category. Businesses that have 2 solid calendar years or 3 total years in existence are classified as established as long as...

Annual Sales or Revenue is Above $150k
Time in business is one factor, but the 2nd is even more important which is annual sales and revenue over $150,000 at least and probably more accurately over $250,000 for the best funding options. Lenders often say $150k, but best results occur when businesses have $250k, so If your business is generating over $250,000 in annual revenue and has 2 to 3 years in existence, then your business will definitely be classified as established and have access to established funding options that are simply not available for startup businesses.

STEP 2: Assess your Credit & Income
What does your credit score look like? Do you have at least a 650 credit score, is it 680 or better? Have you made your payments on time in the last year or two? Do you have a good mix of installment and revolving accounts? What about public records, have you avoided bankruptcy, judgments and tax liens? If your credit sucks, have you found a family member or friend with entrepreneurial ambitions and
© The Business Funding Formula 2017

good credit score of at least a 680, who can join up with you and help to secure funding to launch your venture? Once you have established good credit or have a partner that carries a strong credit profile, move on to the next step which is to assess your income. Do you have w-2 wage income for a job or do you have self employment income for a business that you run and if so what does line 37 show on your adjusted gross income? Do you show enough income to cover your expenses?

A word of wisdom if you have a w-2 job, do not quit it until you secure funding and begin to make solid progress building your business or at least putting together a solid plan. This will help you avoid a lot of headache, I've seen it time and time again, someone needs funding and prematurely quits their job and now struggles to qualify for funding. Keep your job until you get funded and are set to grow your business. We just covered this step in the previous chapter, so jump back to chapter 4 if you would like to review it.

STEP 3: SBA & Secured Funding First

We always start with the best funding options first to see if they are a possibility so even though I'm not always a fan of sba loans we must look at them to see if they are even a possibility. For newer, startup businesses, SBA is limited to the 7(a) program which is extremely difficult to qualify for because it generally will need to be backed up completely with collateral like your 401k, a real estate property with no debt or substantial equity, stocks, bonds or anything easily converted to cash. You will also need a 25 to 30% down payment.

Established businesses with 2 years of profitable business tax returns have a legit chance of securing funding based on 2 years of profitable business tax returns and can secure an sba loan without collateral, but since startups have no established financials they always need to be backed up with collateral. SBA is not the only option that you have that is connected to collateral or security. If you own any vehicle free and clear of debt you can get a loan on the vehicle and receive cash you can use to launch your business. If you have property with no debt or that has equity and you have verifiable income then you may look at securing a home equity line of credit (heloc), this can be one of the most affordable ways to jumpstart your business.

Additionally if you have a 401k/IRA from a previous job you can self direct it to gain access to it tax free in order to start your business or simply get a loan typically up to 50% of the value of your 401k. We will delve into secured funding in chapter 6, sba for startups in chapter 7 and sba for established businesses in chapter 15.

STEP 4: Look at Unsecured Term Loans
Unsecured term loans are a good option to consider, these unsecured loans do not require collateral or security. These are great for startups who don't have collateral or 2 years of profitable business tax returns, as long as you have a decent credit score of 650 or better. 680 and better increases your odds for success and then combine that with some verifiable income that is enough to cover your expenses adequately and you can literally qualify for up to 100k in unsecured term loans. If you need to consolidate your high interest, high balance credit cards to prepare for funding then these unsecured term loans are a great option for that as well. We will look at how these loans work and tackle how to qualify for them in chapter 9.

STEP 5: Traditional Lines of Credit

Traditional lines of credit are kind of like the holy grail of funding for a startup business, because as a line of credit you can use it, pay it down and use it over and over again. What's more when you build a relationship with the lender they will often increase your credit limit over time. These are unsecured lines of credit without collateral or security and generally the rates are manageable and low. Since they are the holy grail, typically the qualifications are more difficult, you generally need at least a 700 fico score and strong income with no late payments in the last 2 to 3 years in order to qualify. Another good option for an entrepreneur and we will break it down into detail in chapter 10.

STEP 6: Revolving Credit Lines/Cards
Revolving credit line, type credit card accounts are an amazingly flexible funding product for businesses, regardless of whether you are a startup or established business it is always helpful to have these accounts. They often come at 0% for 9 to 15 months and then regular credit card rates after that introductory period. They come in personal and business form. The great thing about the business accounts is that they do not report to your personal credit and will actually build your business credit. They are the only business funding that a new startup can secure entirely in the name of the business, and the other great thing about these accounts is that they do not require business or personal financial documentation typically.

If your income is difficult to verify or prove or you have a lot of write off expenses but in reality make more, you can state the appropriate income without having to be scrutinized to pieces with heavy documentation requirements and scrutiny famous by underwriters since the recession. One of the biggest secrets regarding revolving credit lines/cards is that you can actually access up to 90% of the

© The Business Funding Formula 2017

credit limit of each account/card in cash. That's right you can actually pull the cash off these credit cards, and with our secret methodology you can legitimately maintain the 0% rate on these cards while taking out the cash. This particular funding hack took time to learn, but it is a great funding solution. Of course most business expenses can be covered with a card, but there are still a few like payroll and office rent that require cash. Revolving credit lines/cards are a powerful tool especially for startups, we will break down this funding option in Chapter 11.

STEP 7: SBA for Established Businesses
As discussed earlier in this chapter established businesses gain access to some unique funding options that startups do not and one of the biggest benefits of being an established business is that you can qualify for an SBA loan much easier because there are sba loans from 150k and under that do not require collateral with sba. The catch is your last 2 years of business tax returns must show enough profits to cover the expenses of the new loan and you must show enough cashflow to cover your own personal bills.

There are some tricks to how sba calculates your business income so even if you do show a loss on your business tax returns but pay yourself a w-2 salary and have some other expenses like depreciation you may still qualify, we will break this down in chapter 15. As always with sba you must realize that loans can take months although there are some innovative sba lenders that can fund in less than a month if you are aggressive at completing the mountains of paperwork in a timely manner.

STEP 8: Term Loans & Lines of Credit (non SBA)
© The Business Funding Formula 2017

Since sba can still be difficult there have been a number of very competitive, non-sba lenders offering business term loans without needing official collateral to secure the loans. There have also been business lines of credit products created by some non-sba lenders as well. The great thing about these alternative business funding options, available for established businesses with profitable business financials, is that they generally move much quicker than sba. Indeed in some cases you can receive funding in less than a week.

One of these lenders actually set up a business line of credit for our business within 4 business days. 2 to 3 weeks is typical and so much better than waiting forever for sba to get their crap together and let's just say that they request significantly less documentation. Qualifying for these types of loans is similar to sba, however they will do up to $500k without asking for collateral whereas sba is limited to 150k without collateral. A solid option for Established business, check out the details in chapter 16.

STEP 9: Corporate Credit

Corporate or business credit is another one of those holy grail things that entrepreneurs are looking for that seems to be mysterious, but it does exist although differently than most business owners believe. Before the recession, there were some lenders that would lend based on your business credit and would not require the business owner to qualify using personal credit. Those days are pretty much over in terms of securing credit like an american express business card that can be used anywhere american express is accepted, you can however get a $1,500 account set up at Staples and various other vendors if you establish good business credit. Nonetheless, business credit becomes very important for any type of larger funding the more

© The Business Funding Formula 2017

established your business becomes so it is imperative to build your business credit

Established business funding options like SBA, business term loans and business lines of credit all will require a strong business credit score. Business credit will help you secure more funding, help you separate business from personal liabilities, help you secure bigger contracts from larger companies as well as the government and also lead to better funding deals for your business. It is increasingly becoming a requirement to have very good business credit to qualify for an sba loan these days. The corporate credit hacks are found in chapter 17 and it will open a world you never knew existed.

STEP 10: Putting it all Together with Creative financing
Every entrepreneur needs to learn how to secure creative financing. Creative financing might be grabbing an unsecured term loan to pay down your high interest, balance credit cards which will then allow you to qualify for a traditional line of credit and some business credit cards. This is how you put it all together. So when we talk about creative financing we're talking about funding combinations, we're talking about building the strongest profile before you apply for funding. Maybe the best example of creative financing is represented with my story in chapter 2 about when I got a heloc to pay of all of my personal debts and then turned that into 40k from my cars which were paid off in the home equity line of credit and then used afterwards to secure the cash. As I break down each of these items I will demystify how to qualify, how to prepare for funding and how to become a master of funding to grow your business to levels you never thought possible.

STEP 11: Funding Rules to Live By
© The Business Funding Formula 2017

Having seen tremendous success in business and epic failure I have a special set of rules that I created so that when entrepreneurs secure funding, afterwards they are able to make good decisions I wish I had these rules in my possession several years ago! There are also some simple things you can do to manager your payments and utilize your funding to scale up your business, so this is an essential step for overall success..

Funding with Terrible Credit
I have mentioned this in previous chapters, and I will continue to mention it, during the recession I had horrific credit, there was no lender that would've touched me with a 10 foot pole so for all of you out there who say my credit stinks, I'm screwed and I'm not going to get funding. There is a simple solution and it is to find one family member or friend and share your business plan with them and invite them to join you (as long as they have that 680+ credit score). You have to tell them the truth that they are taking on risk, but as long as you give them compensation, equity and a dream to be a part of your business, it's a lot easier for them to co-sign for funding and join your business than to ask them for 50k from their 401k, right?

If you're saying no, my family and friends will not do that for me, then I've got bad news: you are most likely going to fail in your business. If you can't convince one person you know who has good credit to join your business, then you are clearly not committed and 100% vested in making your venture succeed. I have seen so many all the way committed entrepreneurs who have been my clients, and any that are truly serious about their business have almost always found a credit partner within days and went on to secure funding and grow and develop a great business.
© The Business Funding Formula 2017

There is Always a Funding Solution

The Business Funding Formula is built to find a solution for every focused entrepreneur who has a dream of changing the world with their unique product or service. For so many of them it starts with the funding necessary to catapult their fledgling business to the levels of respectability and profit that they desire. By continuing with the funding formula as their startup business grows into an established business they then have the opportunity to grow their business into something more, something legendary…

To find out how much funding you can qualify for, go to www.LeoKanell.com and we will tell you within 24 hours what your Custom Funding Plan might look like for free.

Chapter 6: Secured Funding (Do you have Collateral?)

Secured vs Unsecured

Ok my entrepreneurial friends let's take a look at the 2 financing types available in your business and life: they are secured and unsecured financing. I have covered this some, but to clarify secured funding is any type of loan or line of credit backed with collateral in which if you do not make your payment the lender can take the collateral and sell it to minimize their loss. Unsecured funding of course is much higher risk because there is no collateral or security to protect the lender in case you don't' make payment. Whenever I explain this to entrepreneurs there seems to often be an aha moment where you realize what it's like to be on the other end of the funding transaction.

Imagine if it were your own money that you were lending out, heck if it's my money I would certainly prefer to lend out my money with some collateral backing up the loan as security in case my borrower fails to repay the loan. And if I'm going to lend out my own money without security or collateral you can be damned sure I'm going to charge a higher interest rate to compensate for the fact that if my borrower defaults I have absolutely no collateral to minimize my losses. This should really open your eyes to the fact that lending involves risk and hopefully will put your mind in the right state to understand how grateful you should be that unsecured money exists.

So that said, let's dig into secured and collateralized loans in this chapter and look at what options exist and how you can best manage these secured funding options. Even though SBA startup loans almost

© The Business Funding Formula 2017

always involve collateral we will wait to discuss that option in depth in the next chapter, so for this chapter we will become one with the different secured funding options available to entrepreneurs.

Collateral Types

So there are some different types of secured loans that involve specific and unique collateral types that we will break down right now. They are real estate, vehicles and 401ks/IRA's. Let's break down how each one works and how each one can be used as a funding tool to jumpstart your business.

Real Estate Free and Clear or with Equity

I realize that many new entrepreneurs do not have property that they own free and clear and for those that do, there may be this romantic notion inside of you saying, no I don't want to add debt to my property I'd rather get some regular business funding. Reality is that if you secure a home equity line of credit for any property that you own free and clear you will not find a lower, cheaper financing option than that. So if you own property free and clear your best financing option is to secure a heloc. It will require verifiable income to qualify for a home equity line of credit.

A few years ago when I was starting one of my first companies I had bought a house in foreclosure, fixed it up and I had some equity in it, so I got a home equity line of credit in order to start my business, it was a great idea, simply tap into home equity that wasn't making me a dime and use it to grow my business and make a great return on the money. In order to secure a home equity line of credit this is typically a product that the bank or credit union that you bank at is going to be your best bet, they will need you to have documented, verifiable income in order to qualify for the line, so as long as your income is high enough to cover the new payment which is usually a very cheap and affordable rate and payment then you will be set to get the money your business needs.

Helocs as they are commonly referred to can be very useful especially because they are an affordable option with the flexibility of being a credit line that you can use and pay down and use over and over again. A Mortgage Debt Ratio of 35% to 40% max will be required and probably 45% to 50% of your total debt ratio will be required on top of that.

To calculate mortgage debt ratio let's look at an example, let's say that your monthly verifiable income with your last 2 pay stubs shows $5,000 per month. Your max Mortgage Debt Ratio AKA Top end debt ratio is your monthly mortgage payments divided by your gross monthly income so if your income is 5k per month then if your local bank/credit union had a max mortgage debt ratio of 35% that would mean 35% of 5k would be your max, that is in this example, $1,750.

So your current first mortgage and new Heloc 2nd mortgage payment could not be higher than $1,750. So if you in this example are paying $1,500 per month on a first mortgage, then you could add a new 2nd mortgage Heloc monthly payment of $250 which might get you $25k to $35k depending on your bank or credit union.

To calculate your total debt ratio, let's return to this example. So let's say your 1st mortgage payment is $1,500, you are approved for a new 2nd mortgage Heloc for another $250, and then you have auto loan payments of $500 plus another $250 in minimum monthly credit card payments, that would mean your total debt ratio is about $2,500 all of

© The Business Funding Formula 2017

your minimum monthly payments that show up on your credit report divided by your gross monthly income which in this case was 5k, so $2,500 divided by $5,000 would give you a total AKA bottom debt ratio of 50%, for many banks you may qualify for a heloc 2nd mortgage. So on occasion when you get a Heloc as I did several years ago, your bank or credit union may tell you that the only way they will give you the heloc is if you pay off your other debts like credit cards, auto loans and/or educational loans.

Back to my personal story this is exactly happened to me, I was offered a home equity line of credit and yet the lender required me to pay off all of my personal debts including my credit cards & vehicle loans, so this was good it was going to save me some money.

But it was not going to leave me a cent that I could put towards my business. So now what do I do? That brings us to the next section of Secured Loans, Vehicle Loans.

Vehicles & Trucks
Again your local bank or credit union is almost always your best option as you already have a relationship with the bank or credit union and they should be more likely to push your deal through. You will need documented income to qualify so if you are employed that means last year's W2 and your last 2 pay stubs, if you are self employed then you will need your last 2 years of personal/business tax returns and a year to date P&L.

Your total debt ratio will most likely need to be at 50% or below to qualify so again if the new vehicle loan and all of your other minimum monthly payments on your credit report add up to $2,500 and then that number is divided by your gross monthly income in our continuing example let's say it is $5,000 then 2.5k divided by 5k is 50% and you should be able to qualify. Oddly enough with these types of loans I have seen more success with credit unions than with banks, so if your bank denies you, I suggest you go to a local credit union in that case.

Always Limit your hard inquiries

401k's/IRA's

Let's jump into the 401k/IRA option, there are two ways you can turn your 401k/IRA into an asset to fuel your new business. This must generally be a 401k or IRA from a previous job, if your 401k or IRA is with your current employer then it may not be eligible. The first thing that you can do with a 401k/IRA is you can choose to self direct your IRA, by self directing your IRA you can become the decider of what your IRA is invested in, to self direct it you will set up an LLC and have the entity invest it into your business. You will need a professional IRA self directing company to set it up.

The second way to utilize your 401k/IRA while still keeping it as a retirement account and avoiding having to pay obligatory taxes is to actually secure a loan with your IRA/401k as collateral while still keeping the IRA invested in the market to continue its growth. This is a very affordable option, again we have some proven contacts found at www.BusinessFundingFormula.com that I have personally worked with and do a very good job of putting your IRA to work well for your business, their fees are also very competitive.

Let's talk about the qualifying factors needed to secure a loan from a 401k/IRA, I once had a client Veronica who really wanted to start a business, her credit score wasn't great, she didn't have any assets, but she did have an IRA, so even though there were no other possible options for her to secure funding for her business, she was able to qualify for an IRA loan and began to build her new business with that tool.

To find out how much funding you can qualify for, go to www.LeoKanell.com and we will tell you within 24 hours what your Custom Funding Plan might look like for free.

Chapter 7: Is SBA Possible for a Startup

SBA is not Lending, Just Backing Local Lenders
SBA stands for Small Business Administration which is a government backed entity sponsored by the federal government in the US to help small businesses. SBA doesn't' actually lend money to businesses, in fact they actually back up anywhere from about 65% to 90% of the money that banks and credit unions lend to small businesses for SBA specific loans. So if you are looking for funding from the SBA, you will find it by going to your local bank or credit union.

One trend that has continued after the great recession has been that overwhelmingly banks are lending to the bigger businesses not necessarily the "small businesses." Bigger businesses have more income, cashflow and assets so it certainly makes sense that they spend most of their time and resources securing larger loan amounts for these businesses. The other trend is that banks rarely lend outside of sba loans when it comes to larger loan amounts to businesses, there is so much lower risk for banks and credit unions to simply lend mostly sba backed loans. In this chapter we will delve into startup sba funding options with the SBA, for more established business funding with SBA I will cover that in chapter 15. For all things SBA go to www.SBA.gov Here we go.

The 7(a) is the only SBA startup Funding Program

SBA offers really one major startup funding program and it is designated as the 7(a) program. The uses of the loan are purchase or expand a business, buy inventory or equipment, working capital and refinance debt. As a startup or newer business without 2 years of proven financials you will only qualify 99.99% of the time for an asset backed sba 7(a) startup loan for your new business. So as stated in the previous chapter, acceptable collateral might be real estate owned free and clear or property with significant equity in it or some newer equipment that the business needs. For most new business owners, your primary residence where you live if it has decent equity will be a potential piece of collateral for an sba 7(a) loan. I have seen sba accept 401k/IRA's as well as expensive equipment owned free and clear or bought new. So if you do actually possess these acceptable collateral types that is still not going to be enough, the majority of sba lending banks and credit unions will also require a down payment. So if you need 100k, typically a 25% down payment is required by SBA in order to secure that 7(a) loan.

A friend and client of mine Mike started a Scooter's coffee shop franchise and the SBA lender asked him to pledge his large 401k from his previous job as collateral, even with strong credit, collateral like his 401k and the new equipment that he purchased for the coffee shop, it still ended up taking about 6 months to secure the loan he needed for the business and at the same time it still did not allow him working capital for marketing and payroll. Our funding team helped him with working capital.

The bottom line is that sba 7a loans are very difficult to obtain, often take several months, require mountains of paperwork, require you to sign in blood and pledge every asset you have and will require a down payment as a cherry on top of your sba 7a sundae! The worst part is that many entrepreneurs spend months going through the process only to receive a decline after months and hundreds of hours of work in the process, I do not recommend SBA for new businesses.

Below is a table with a breakdown of SBA's 3 main programs.

Small Business Administration (SBA) Financing Table

Loan Type	SBA 504	SBA 7(A) Loans	SBA Express
Use it for	Purchase equipment or real estate (no refinancing) Construction and renovation	Purchase or expand a business Purchase equipment or inventory Working capital Refinance debt	Working capital Purchase equipment Purchase vehicles or inventory

© The Business Funding Formula 2017

Benefits			
	Longer maturity than conventional loan	Longer maturity than conventional loan	Longer maturity than some conventional loans
	Lower down payments on fixed assets	Lower down payments on fixed assets	Easier qualification than a Conventional loan
	Easier qualification than a conventional loan	Easier qualification than a conventional loan	
Amount	$350,000 minimum, no maximum	$350,000- $5,000,000	$25,000-$350,000
Terms	Up to 2 years interim construction period 7-10 years on equipment 10-20 years on real estate	Up to 7 years for working capital Up to 10 years for equipment or business acquisition Up to 25 years for real estate	7-year term with first-year revolving option and Balance amortized across the remainder of the term

7(m) Microloan

SBA does have one additional program known as the microloan program where supposedly these microlenders will offer an sba loan to new businesses up to $50k. The average microloan is about 13k, and the paperwork and other requirements are still very difficult and time consuming for such small amounts of 13k as the average loan. There is a strong focus on funding minority or traditionally disadvantaged entrepreneurs with this program, if you have the patience and time, this is an option, but again I cannot in good conscience advocate much for it as a legit funding option as the amounts are small and the time spent could be spent building your business and there are so many superior funding options.

SBA Startup Funding is Rare, Difficult and Time Consuming

My focus with the business funding formula is to look at whether SBA is a legit option and for 99.99% of startups, I do not believe it is a legit option. For established businesses SBA is a more plausible possibility, but for startups, it is mostly a waste of your very valuable time.

To find out how much funding you can qualify for, go to www.LeoKanell.com and we will tell you within 24 hours what your Custom Funding Plan might look like for free.

Chapter 8: A Trick to Save You Thousands

This One Trick Will Save you Tens of Thousands over a Lifetime
Years ago when I first went through this process I was able to land some secured loans with home equity and with vehicles that I owned free and clear, but when I got to the unsecured business credit lines/cards that did not require collateral I didn't succeed on the level that I wanted.
So I spent countless hours researching and reviewing credit forums, spoke with several lenders and I started to find an interesting pattern that increased funding success at an astounding level.

It's Called Credit Utilization
As a business owner until your company is doing over $50 Million in annual sales your funding will always be connected to your personal credit. Often if you pay all of your accounts on credit like a mortgage, auto loan and credit card on time, you assume that you have strong personal credit. However I soon found out that on time payments

alone weren't enough, then I discovered a huge trick that makes a huge difference and it is called your credit utilization rate.

For every revolving account that you have, like a credit card or credit line it is essential for your balance to limit ratio to be under 45% and if possible under 30%. For example let's say that you have a $10,000 credit card, then you would want your balance to be at $4,500 and if possible around $3,000. 4.5k/10k = 45% and 3k/10k=30%. Maintaining a revolving credit utilization rate below 45% of your credit card limits is a huge key to funding success!

This one trick will keep your credit score high and show lenders that you are a low risk, when you go to a lender asking for money and you have a maxed out credit card, you have to put yourself in the lender's position and see that you are one bad pay day from defaulting on that account and others. It looks like you're tapped out. This one aspect of your personal credit will help you to keep a higher credit score and allow you to qualify for the lowest rates on mortgages, auto loans, business loans, credit cards and every credit account for the rest of your life. This information will save you thousands of dollars if not tens of thousands in lower interest paid out over your lifetime! So where I may have only qualified for 15k in funding now I was able to secure funding of 50k or more at favorable terms.

Another key moment was when I learned that if you are in the startup phase you can't go to one lender and ask them for one large credit line or loan without having 2 years of profitable business tax returns and some strong collateral. That led to a huge breakthrough where I learned that if you asked for smaller loan amounts or credit lines from 5 to 6 lenders that with those smaller amounts being added up I could

© The Business Funding Formula 2017

then secure the amount of cumulative capital that I needed. The end result was that we were able to creatively secure the most affordable financing possible to fuel the growth of our business, we were able to buy the inventory we needed, we were able to put together a superior brick and mortar office, hire new staff and take our business to levels we would never have hit without that capital. That is the result that every entrepreneur is looking for.

Before Applying for Funding Do This (the Story of Karen)
 Karen is a world renowned holistic health teacher, she teaches people how to be healthy, she's a remarkable woman full of endless energy, has 8 kids and has built an incredible following. However at one point she hit a ceiling and was unable to grow her business any further without some capital. She went to her bank where she had built a relationship and figured that she would easily qualify for $50,000 in funding. To her surprise her bank turned her down, but her bank had heard about my funding formula and suggested that she look at that as a solution. Karen is an incredibly intelligent woman, but had never been taught about the secret of paying down credit card balances before asking for funding, she also didn't know the exact lenders to see where she would have the greatest chance for funding success.

Before applying for funding pull up your credit report at CreditCheckTotal.com or Experian.com and check to make sure all of your credit card balances are reporting below 50% of the limit on each account and truly reporting that. Just because you paid them down last week doesn't' mean they have updated the new, lower balance with all 3 credit bureaus.

© The Business Funding Formula 2017

Back to my friend Karen, after going through the funding formula steps and getting her credit card balances paid down we created a custom funding plan and she was able to secure $59,000 in business and personal credit lines/cards at 0% for the first year. What a difference it made before beginning the process she had been turned down at all of the other lenders and with the funding formula she had success.

HERE'S WHAT'S IMPORTANT
The results brought about by her funding have been absolutely incredible, her website has been upgraded and looks like a million bucks was spent on it, she is doing live events all over the country and the world with the affordable marketing she can do thanks to her funding. She has published books, a huge following I really admire her a lot, but the coolest part is that she was able to breakthrough to the good life by using the right funding steps and one of the key steps is to look at your revolving credit usage before applying for funding.

What if You Lack Cash to Pay down High Balance Credit Cards
This is a great question, now that you know this big secret, what do you do if you lack the cash to pay down your high balance credit cards? Are you destined to be without capital? As I always say there is always a funding solution so in the next chapter we will cover how unsecured term loans can be the solution to pay down your high balance credit cards.

To find out how much funding you can qualify for, go to www.LeoKanell.com and we will tell you within 24 hours what your Custom Funding Plan might look like for free.

© The Business Funding Formula 2017

Chapter 9: Unsecured Term Loans

What are Unsecured Term Loans

OK, so if the SBA & Secured loan options weren't' workable solutions for you or if they were, but you still need additional capital for your business, then let's take a look at one of my favorite options for securing additional capital. During the time of the recession, as banks pulled back lending, a new type of loan program was developed by various organizations in which consumers can secure a nice 3, 5, or 7 year term loan through peer to peer lending done by some lenders that have literally funded billions of dollars in very useful loans.

To be clear these are going to be personal loans that do NOT require collateral which is cool because for a startup business, essentially SBA and secured loans are all offered only if you have collateral and assets to pledge in order to secure the loan. Well for a lot of dynamic business owners, they may not have any collateral growing on a tree. So no collateral needed, they do however need verifiable personal income.

So just to reiterate, these are unsecured loans which means that you do not need collateral and what that really means is that of course without collateral there is higher risk and so the rates logically will be higher than your 4% mortgage backed by your house. It's so important to understand that first and the 2nd thing to understand is yes, the rates are higher, but so what you should be making 100 to 200% or more on the money and so even at a high rate of 20% it doesn't matter because you are getting 100% ROI on the money and more than covering the cost and the loan payback.

© The Business Funding Formula 2017

Use a Term Loan to Pay down those High Interest Credit Cards!
Before we dive into this very useful lending program, first allow me to point out if you are very interested in the credit lines as a solution for your new business. Do NOT skip ahead to that section because often in order to qualify for funding you may need to secure a term loan in order to pay down some of your credit card balances so that you will be able to qualify. Often the term loan is something that you will get done first before moving on to the credit line portion of the funding formula.

Ok, so that said, let's first look at a real life example of how these types of loans can be used to accomplish what you want. 2 of my clients Erin & Steve wanted to start a hot dog franchise, and the needed 50k to 60k in order to get their business going. My daughter dances competitively with their granddaughter so it was really important to help them find a funding solution. *If you want to watch Erin's experience go to YouTube and type in "Leo Kanell, Erin Massa."* The problem was that they had maxed out credit that needed to be paid down, and they didn't have extra money to pay down those credit card balances so that they could qualify for unsecured credit lines, they also didn't have assets that they could use in order to secure some secured loans or SBA loans. Maxed out credit cards as discussed in the previous chapter will kill your funding.

Fortunately thanks to the unsecured term loan program they were able to qualify for $20k and with that money they were able to pay down some maxed out credit cards to below 50% of the limits and position themselves so that they could qualify for not just 50k, but over 80k in unsecured credit lines/cards at 0% interest for the first year. What great people who really deserved the opportunity, the business funding formula helped them to accomplish that. The best part is that they just opened a second location and were able to tap into their revolving credit lines again in order to expand from 1 location to a second. That is the power of the funding formula!

How do you Qualify?
So what does it take to qualify. Typically you need to have a minimum credit score of at least 650 with all 3 of your credit scores with all 3 credit bureaus: Experian, Equifax & Transunion. I have found the best credit reporting service to show accurate scores and credit reporting histories with all 3 credit bureaus to be www.CreditCheckTotal.com or www.ScoreSense.com. Their credit monitoring services are NOT a hard inquiry, but rather a soft inquiry. Before starting this process check your credit reports and scores with all 3 credit bureaus, know what is on there, if there are small errors, try and work those out with creditors before applying, if nothing can be changed with the creditor then simply move forward.

Now, what does it take credit wise to qualify, typically these personal term lenders want to see a 650 credit score and some account history meaning a car loan that you've had for a couple of years and a credit card or two for 2 or 3 years. In addition to the age of a loan or a credit account, the amount also helps play a part, a car loan with an initial amount above $10,000 is helpful and a $5,000 credit card limit also helps.

Unsecured term lenders don't want to see a lot of credit inquiries in the past 3 to 6 months and they also don't want to see tax liens or

© The Business Funding Formula 2017

bankruptcies on your public record. They also do not want to see judgments or collections, if you have them on your credit report then they definitely need to have been paid, if they are open and not paid, they should be less than 1k and hopefully are over 2 years old in order to get approvals. Bankruptcies probably need to be at least 5 years old and you need to have re-established good payment histories since the bk. If is also important to have gotten any old accounts that were included in the bk removed from your report. The majority of these lenders in order to pre-approve you will actually do a soft pull instead of a hard pull, a soft pull has no negative impact on your credit while a hard pull can have a negative impact on your credit. Throughout this process you will need to keep track of the importance of limiting your credit pulls. This is definitely one of the positive aspects of these unsecured term loans that most will do a soft pull and typically only make it hard if they final approve your loan.

Income documentation: These lenders love to lend out to borrowers with w2 income. So for most of you as borrowers you will have your previous year's W2 and your last 2 pay stubs to show verifiable income. Lenders will sometimes check with your employer and confirm your employment as well as verify with the IRS your W2 info. Of course they prefer that you have had the same job for at least 2 years, but as long as your current job is in the same line of work as your previous job then you will be just fine as long as your income is still high enough for you to qualify. They will also accept a signed offer letter for any new job or employment that you have recently secured.

If you are self employed and already running your business or receive 1099 income, then the lender will ask for your last 2 years of personal and business tax returns (if not filed on your schedule C of your personal tax return) they may also need a year to date Profit and Loss showing your business net income, but rarely ask for it. For a self employed borrower they will generally go off of your adjusted gross income which is usually the last line of page 1 of your personal tax return on the federal form 1040, which is line 37. In the field where it asks for other income, if you have other income like rent income from a rental property, social security income, alimony, disability income or any other type of verifiable income, LIST IT. Minimum income to qualify for an unsecured term loan is typically at least $45,000 depending on your debt ratio.

Debt Ratio: Most of these lenders will want to see that your current debt ratio is below 45%, and some will want it below 35%, your debt ratio has always been somewhat secretive with lenders in terms of how it is calculated, but it is not a rocket science calculation, it is simply calculated. Every minimum monthly payment showing up on your credit report divided by your monthly gross income is your debt ratio. So let's say all of my monthly payments on my credit report are 3 credit card payments, 2 car loan payments, 2 student loan payments and 1 mortgage. To calculate my debt ratio I will simply add up all minimum monthly payments which will be listed on your credit report, all of them and divide it by your gross monthly income before taxes. Do NOT add in utility or other payments that are not showing up on your credit report.

Let's say my payments add up to $2,000 and my annual income is about $60,000 or $5,000 per month, then I will divide $2,000 by $5,000 and get 40%, that is my debt ratio. Most often the only types of payments showing up on your credit report will be mortgages, vehicle loans, recreational loans (like boats, motorcycles, rv's etc.), credit

© The Business Funding Formula 2017

cards, lines of credit, some business credit lines/cards and of course education/student loans. To review, you want your debt ratio to be under 45 and if possible under 35% to qualify, although if you are just over, still apply.

So after you complete your online loan application, next the lender will ask for you to upload your loan documents for final review before they will fund the loan. Common docs requested will be: Last year's W2, last 2 pay stubs (if employed) or (last 2 yrs personal/biz tax returns if self employed & a YTD P&L), copy of your driver's license, passport and birth certificate, copy of utility bill matching your address. If you are missing a document from this list, worry not, simply call the lender's customer service and they will tell you what will work.

Typical Terms for Unsecured Term Loans

Rates are incredibly low from 6% to 9% with the top tier unsecured term loans and with 2nd tier and beyond rates typically go from 9 to 19%. Tier 3 for lower credit can be higher.

Terms are typically 3, 5, or 7 year terms.

Loan amounts are from $5,000 to $100,000 for tier 1 if you have enough income you can qualify for larger amounts and monthly payments are low and affordable. For example a $50k loan will carry a $800 monthly payment and a $100k loan will have a $1,600 monthly payment. Tier 2 and 3 lenders typically will max out at a loan amount of $40,000.

Where do you Get Unsecured Term Loans?

There are a number of lenders that offer unsecured term loans including banks and several online lenders, just to give you an idea of one of these lenders go to www.Prosper.com and you can apply for an unsecured term loan at that site. For a full breakdown of the very best unsecured term lenders and products and to find out how much funding you can qualify for, go to www.LeoKanell.com and we will tell you within 24 hours what your Custom Funding Plan might look like for free.

.

Chapter 10: Traditional Lines of Credit

What are Traditional Lines of Credit
Traditional lines of credit are probably the most flexible and useful unsecured funding available today. There are several reasons why, they are revolving lines of credit with easily accessible cash access via bank transfer or check, the rates are lower than credit line/card rates overall and since they are lines of credit they can be used, paid down and used over and over again. Monthly payments are also affordable and generally are calculated at 2 to 3% of the balance is the monthly payment so a $25,000 line of credit fully utilized would have a monthly payment of $500 to $750 or so.

These lines of credit are personal, we will be covering business lines of credit in chapter 16. In order to qualify for business term loans and lines of credit entirely in the name of the business you will need 2 years of profitable business tax returns. The lines of credit referred to in this chapter are personal in nature and would be available to newer entrepreneurs who can qualify for these lines of credit.
© The Business Funding Formula 2017

So what does it take to qualify.

Typically you need to have a minimum credit score of at least 700 with all 3 of your credit scores with all 3 credit bureaus: Experian, Equifax & Transunion. I have found the best credit reporting service to show accurate scores and credit reporting histories with all 3 credit bureaus to be www.CreditCheckTotal.com or www.ScoreSense.com. Their credit monitoring services are NOT a hard inquiry, but rather a soft inquiry. Before starting this process check your credit reports and scores with all 3 credit bureaus, know what is on there, if there are small errors, try and work those out with creditors before applying, if nothing can be changed with the creditor then simply move forward.

Now, what does it take credit wise to qualify, typically these personal traditional lines of credit lenders want to see a 700 credit score and some account history meaning a car loan that you've had for a couple of years and a credit card or two for 2 or 3 years. In addition to the age of a loan or a credit account, the amount also helps play a part, a car loan with an initial amount above $20,000 is helpful and a $8,000 credit card limit also helps. They also do not want to see a lot of inquiries and new accounts within the last 18 months, especially newer revolving accounts like other lines of credit or credit cards.

Traditional lines of credit lenders have higher expectations than unsecured term loan lenders in that they generally do not have any tolerance for any public records like judgments, bankruptcies or tax liens, they also expect lower debt to income ratios below 40% typically.

Income documentation: These lenders love to lend out to borrowers with w2 income. So for most of you as borrowers you will have your previous year's W2 and your last 2 paystubs to show verifiable income. Lenders will often check with your employer and confirm your employment as well as verify with the IRS your W2 info. Of course they prefer that you have had the same job for at least 2 years, but as long as your current job is in the same line of work as your previous job then you will be just fine as long as your income is still high enough for you to qualify.

If you are self employed and already running your business or receive 1099 income, then the lender will ask for your last 2 years of personal and business tax returns (if not filed on your schedule C of your personal tax return) they may also need a year to date Profit and Loss showing your business net income. For a self employed borrower they will generally go off of your adjusted gross income which is usually the last line of page 1 of your personal tax return, line 37. In the field where it asks for other income, if you have other income like rent income from a rental property or any other type of verifiable income, LIST IT. A significant difference with traditional lines of credit lenders vs unsecured term loan lenders is that they want higher incomes of at least 70k or greater depending on your debt ratio. They do have one exception, if you own your home free and clear or have significant real estate equities, 401k/IRA and other assets then those can act as an exception to requiring higher incomes.

Debt Ratio: Most of these lenders will want to see that your current debt ratio is below 40%, and some will prefer it below 30%, your debt ratio has always been somewhat secretive with lenders in terms of how it is calculated, but it is not a rocket science calculation, it is simply

© The Business Funding Formula 2017

calculated. Every minimum monthly payment showing up on your credit report divided by your monthly gross income is your debt ratio.

So let's say all of my monthly payments on my credit report are 3 credit card payments, 2 car loan payments, 2 student loan payments and 1 mortgage, well to get my debt ratio I will simply add up all minimum monthly payments which will be listed on your credit report, all of them except your mortgage and divide it by your gross monthly income before taxes. Do NOT add in utility or other payments that are not showing up on your credit report. Let's say my payments add up to $2,000 and my annual income is about $60,000 or $5,000 per month, then I will divide $2,000 by $5,000 and get 40%, that is my debt ratio. Most often the only types of payments showing up on your credit report will be mortgages, vehicle loans, recreational loans (like boats, motorcycles, rv's etc.), credit cards, lines of credit, some business credit lines/cards and of course education/student loans.

To review, you want your debt ratio to be under 40 and if possible under 30% to qualify for larger limits, although if you are just over those ratios, still apply as you have nothing to lose. So after you complete your online loan application, next the lender will ask for you to upload your loan documents for final review before they will fund the loan. Common docs requested will be: Last year's W2, last 2 pay stubs (if employed) or (last 2 yrs personal/biz tax returns if self employed & a YTD P&L), copy of your driver's license, passport and birth certificate, copy of utility bill matching your address. If you are missing a document from this list, worry not, simply call the lender's customer service and they will tell you what will work.

Typical Terms for Traditional Lines of Credit
© The Business Funding Formula 2017

Rates are incredibly low from 6 to 11% for most traditional lines of credit not secured by any collateral. Terms are typically several years meaning that you can use your line of credit and pay it down and use it over and over again for years to come. Typically after you are approved and have provided all income docs and other requests, lenders will not ask you for income and other documentation over the years to maintain your line of credit.

Traditional lines of credit can have limits as large as $100,000, but most are limited to $25k to $30k. if you have enough income you can qualify for larger amounts and monthly payments are low and affordable. For example a $25k line of credit will carry a $500 to $750 monthly payment.

Where do you Get Traditional Lines of Credit?
There are a number of lenders that offer unsecured term loans including banks and several credit unions that are licensed in all 50 states, just to give you an idea of one of these lenders go to www.WellsFargo.com and you can apply for a traditional line of credit at that site although many of these lenders may require you to set up a bank account with them first.
 For a full breakdown of the very best traditional lines of credit and products and to find out how much funding you can qualify for, go to www.LeoKanell.com and we will tell you within 24 hours what your Custom Funding Plan might look like for free.

Chapter 11: Revolving Credit Lines/Cards

What are Revolving Credit Lines/Cards

Thus far we have covered some excellent startup funding options including: SBA loans, secured loans which both require collateral, next we looked at the powerful option of securing unsecured term loans and traditional lines of credit that are both great tools. Now we are crossing into what is arguably the most powerful, easiest to qualify for and most flexible tool to get your startup funded and growing. It's time for unsecured credit lines.

One thing I want to point out is that if your credit is less than perfect and you're on the edge of qualifying. You may still qualify, you don't have anything to lose by going through the funding process and trying to secure capital, if you don't get enough, then of course you can move towards finding a credit partner to secure the rest of the capital needed. So all that said whether you qualify for bank or sba loans, unsecured term loans, or traditional lines of credit, regardless of whether you qualify for those loan types; in reality every new entrepreneur should secure unsecured credit lines. Allow me to explain the features of these credit lines.

- Affordable Monthly payment, calculated at just 2% of the balance you use, (example, 50k = 1k monthly payment)
- An affordable monthly payment that gives you time to generate a return on the money. Incredibly affordable compared to the daily payment loans.
- They are credit lines, you only pay on them if you actually use them, use and pay them down and they will benefit you for the life of your business.

- No Collateral or income documentation required is a huge advantage compared to bank and sba loans which require significant documentation.
- 0% rate for the first 9 to 15 months, so that means 100% of your monthly payment the first year goes completely to principal with no interest, in the 2nd year the rates are from 8 to 21%.
- You can secure business credit lines that do not report to your personal credit.
- Funding available within 2-4 weeks instead of waiting for months for a NO at your bank.

Let's clear up any confusion regarding what credit lines/cards are. An unsecured credit line is not a traditional bank line of credit, a traditional bank line of credit almost always requires significant collateral and years of very profitable personal/business tax returns, they also do not have a 0% rate the first year. A traditional business bank line of credit is almost always secured to expensive, newer equipment and/or a free and clear piece of real estate or investment account. Of course as we discussed in the previous chapter, personal traditional lines of credit can be unsecured and require income documentation.

An unsecured credit line is just that, it is unsecured and as we have reviewed they are the perfect financial tool for an entrepreneur due to their flexibility and the fact that they are the easiest biz financing product available in today's post recession market. So what are they exactly? They are also a type of business credit card and personal credit card, forget everything you've ever heard about credit cards and the negative connotations given to them. With my proven methods you can make these unsecured credit lines/cards exactly what you need and in most cases as a new business owner these credit lines/cards will be the very best financing you can qualify for. The best unsecured credit lines are often business credit lines/cards since they do not report to personal credit, however the requirements are different and require a foundation that I will cover in this chapter.

At the end of the day there only 2 real differences between a traditional line of credit and unsecured credit lines, the first is a traditional line of credit charges you interest from day one and most of the unsecured credit lines/cards I recommend charge 0% for the first year. The 2nd major difference and the one most people are confused about is the ability to access cash. The majority of business purchases can be made with plastic in today's technologically driven world, but some things like payroll and lease rent payments do require cash, and most people are not aware that there are methods to access 90% of your credit lines as cash while maintaining the 0% introductory rate.

Bottom line, at the end of the day entrepreneurs should secure unsecured credit lines/cards and utilize them wisely since they are the most flexible business finance product available and more importantly are the easiest to qualify for. Most importantly they are affordable.

How do you Qualify?

The Requirements are:
- 680 + score, no late payments or collections in the last 6 months.
- No judgments, collections or tax liens that are not paid.

- At least one credit line/card with a $2,500 limit and at least a 1 year history
- Helps to have an installment loan like a car loan or mortgage that is at least 5k, education loans do not help.
- Small amount of credit inquiries over the past 3 to 6 months.

The great thing about the requirements for unsecured credit lines is that it is significantly easier to qualify for credit lines vs Bank loans/sba loans and secured loans. So what do you do if you don't have a 680 credit score? It's a heck of alot easier to find someone with a good credit score than it is to find someone to give you 50k to 100k in hard earned money as a loan.

Every friend or client I've ever known that was serious about their business was not going to let anything stop them from starting a business. As such they often are able to find one friend, one family member or even a stranger with good credit in order to secure enough money to start their business, and they do it with unsecured credit lines.

The most important qualifying factor to secure unsecured credit lines/cards begins with your personal credit report, so if you haven't been monitoring your personal credit it's time to learn a little bit more about your personal credit. The tips alone are extremely valuable and not well known and understood by most of the tens of millions of adults in the US that have a personal credit report on file with the 3 main credit bureaus: Experian, Equifax and Transunion.

By understanding your credit better and how lenders use it to make lending decisions can save you thousands if not hundreds of
© The Business Funding Formula 2017

thousands over the years. Follow the tips and you will improve your financial situation dramatically, and for our purposes it can be the difference between not only a lower rate, but an approval versus a loan denial. Begin by going to www.CreditCheckTotal.com and set up a credit monitoring service (if you haven't already). The first thing that you'll want to do is get the entire pdf file and print it out or save it as a pdf to review it.

How to review your Credit Check Total report
At the top of the report is your profile, it is important for your name and address to all match up, lenders like it when everything matches up, so you want to have the same address listed on each credit bureau report and your correct name listed on it as well. If it is not updated, then you will want to update the profiles for each credit bureau by contacting them and updating the right address. If you recently moved then you will want to use your previous address and just make sure the mail forwards to your new address. New address apps often are declined as they look like identity theft when they may in fact not be. Next, the summary of the report is listed with your real estate, revolving (credit lines/cards), installment (vehicle & student loans) and collections. Pay attention to the delinquent count which is listed on the summary for your report. Obviously you want to avoid delinquent or collection accounts.

Public Records: This is an important area, you definitely want the public record area to be clean and empty with nothing there. Public records can be everything from bankruptcy, tax liens and judgments. Of course bankruptcy and tax liens can certainly lower the amounts you will be approved and so let's break them down a little. An open chapter 13 bankruptcy will lead to automatic denials, in my opinion a chapter 13 bankruptcy that is open will hurt your credit for longer than a chapter 7. If you have filed a chapter 7, then you need to pay attention to the creditors/lenders that you included in the bk, those are creditors you are likely to be declined with in the future.

Tax liens can also be approval killers unless they are small like under $1,000. Judgments have a similar negative impact, if they are large then they will bring automatic denials, if they are under $1,000 then you may still get approvals. It the judgment has been paid off and is reporting that it has been paid and released, likewise a tax lien then you can still qualify for credit line/card accounts, but if they are not paid and released then you are likely to be automatically declined.

Inquiries: the credit inquiries on all 3 of your credit reports are extremely important when it comes to securing credit lines in particular. The lower the amount of inquiries over the last 4 to 6 months the higher your likelihood of securing credit lines will be. Now all inquiries are not created equally, mortgage inquiries and car loan inquiries are not as detrimental as credit line/card inquiries. If you are trying to get unsecured credit lines and have a bunch of inquiries then that will lower your ability to get approvals.

Credit accounts, next you will see all of the credit accounts that are on your credit report including mortgages, car loans, student loans, credit cards etc. In the top left rectangle of each account you will see a checkmark, gray check marks you will note are good accounts that are closed, green check marks will note that the account is current and open.

Red check marks are the ones to look out for, red check marks mean the account has negative aspects like: 30, 60, 90 day lates and charge offs/collections will of course make an account negative as well.

Obviously you want to have **as few late payments as possible**, especially no late payments over the past 12 months, same with collections, hopefully they are small and paid. If they are older collections it is best not to pay them unless the creditor will agree to provide you a letter explaining specifically that the collection or negative account has been satisfied and can be deleted from your credit report, otherwise if you pay the credit it will actually show a recent delinquency and lower your score.

Qualifying Accounts: Unsecured Credit Card lenders are looking for established account history in particular, for example if someone has a 740 credit score and only 2 $500 credit card accounts with 6 months history vs. someone with a 690 score who has 4 $5,000 credit cards with a 5 year history who do you think will get approved for credit lines? The lower score report with a thicker, stronger history in terms of larger account balances & limits and more time will always do better than someone with a high score and limited credit.

A good rule of thumb is that a lender wants to see at least a $5,000 credit card limit account with at least 2 to 3 years of history on it and an installment loan like a car loan with a 3 year history and at least a $8,000 balance or larger. A good mix of revolving (credit card) accounts and installment (vehicle loans & mortgages) are what lenders want, but at a minimum you want to have at least one $5,000 account with a couple year history, the account can be a credit card or installment loan.

Another rule is to carry a balance on your credit card. Think about it, if you are a lender are you going to lend to someone that doesn't carry a credit card balance? Why would you, if they don't carry a balance then as a credit card company you don't make any thing so it is best to have a balance on credit cards, now what is the balance to limit ratio

© The Business Funding Formula 2017

supposed to look like? Here it comes. On credit line/card apps select often when asked if you carry a balance on your credit cards.

BIG KEY, PAY ATTENTION, revolving credit balance to limit ratio aka utilization rate: This is a HUGE FACTOR that we covered in chapter 8 and will again here. It is a big key in determining your credit score and whether a lender will extend unsecured credit lines/card to you. The rule is simple at a minimum you want to have your credit balance to limit ratio on any and all credit cards below 50%, for example, let's say you have a $10,000 credit card limit, you would want your balance to be below $5,000 or 50% on that credit card.

That goes for every and all credit cards on your credit report. Sometimes you might not consider a home depot or store account as a credit card, but that's exactly what they are. Just like a visa or mastercard credit card with a balance and a limit, store credit cards are also revolving accounts that you will want to carry a lower balance with, in order to maximize your credit and funding. 50% is the highest balance you want to carry on a credit card before applying for funding, of course if you can bring it down to 30% that is even better. So what do you do if you have maxed out credit cards which a lot of people do, including aspiring business owners? That is what the unsecured term loans are all about that I discussed in chapter 9. There is a reason why I mentioned paying down credit cards & debt consolidation as one of the top reasons to list in acquiring an unsecured term loan. By utilizing the term loan money you can then pay down your credit card balances to the right amounts.

Let's look at a real life example. One of my good friends & clients had a Home depot card with a $5,000 balance and a $7,000 limit, a

© The Business Funding Formula 2017

Discover card with a $19,000 balance on a $20,000 limit and a Capital One account with a $2,190 balance and a $2,705 limit. So based on what we just reviewed, what are the balances that she would want in order to increase her odds for securing unsecured credit lines?
Well 30% is ideal, but let's say you could only get enough money from a term loan or from moving some money around to get to 50% of the limits. That would mean you would pay down the home depot card by $1,500 to a $3,500 balance on a 7k limit, pay down discover by 9k to a 10k balance on a 20k limit and $840 to pay down the Capital One balance, so that is $11,340. to pay down the balances to a 50% limit. Pop quiz, what do you do if you can't pay down your card balances because you can't qualify for a term loan? What about your other credit card balances, let's look at another example where you can find solutions.

Let's say you have 2 $10k credit card limits, both maxed out, but you also have 2 additional 10k limit cards that have a 0 balance. Well you can contact the two 10k limit, 0 balance credit card companies and request a balance transfer of $5,000 from each to pay down the other 10k balance cards each to 5k. Now you will show a total of 4 separate 10k credit limit accounts, with each having a 5k balance. Believe it or not, this actually will make a significant difference in getting approvals and bigger credit lines. It just makes you look so much more responsible and "fundable."

So what happens if you apply for unsecured credit lines with maxed out credit cards? You will be declined most if not all places, when a lender sees that your credit cards are maxed out they know that you are one bad month, emergency or lost job from being unable to pay your bills and defaulting on a lot of credit accounts. After you get your unsecured term loan funded, next you will want to call each credit card company and ask them to update your balance with all 3 credit bureaus as a one time courtesy. It may take a call or two, to get the right person to update it, but rest assured you must wait and verify that the balances are updated by logging into CreditCheckTotal.com to verify that your balances are paid down with all 3 credit bureaus.

Make sure to remember to scroll through the entire report to confirm that the account balances have been paid down and are reporting correctly. Believe me, this is the one time where patience is a virtue that will serve you well.

Review this chapter often, but the overall message is clear, keep your card balances paid down below 50% of the limits and avoid public records and make your payments on time, but the simple key is to keep those balances paid down and your credit score will soar as much as 30 to 50 points when compared to maxed out credit cards and lines paid down below 50%.

Make Your Damn Payments on Time
Since I've looked at tens of thousands of credit reports I have to make this point. It is absolutely ludicrous and I have been shocked and chagrined several times when I have reviewed the credit reports of entrepreneurs looking for money, who for reasons unknown forget to make payments on 2 $30 monthly payments for 2 little credit cards. How that little mishap can derail their funding is a very sad happening.

It has never been easier to make your payments on time, nearly all accounts you acquire on credit can be registered online and more importantly you can turn on automatic minimum monthly payments to ensure that your payments are made in a timely manner. So if you know you're going to get funding now or in the future set up automatic minimum monthly payments. It's even more baffling to me when you take into account that late payments on personal credit do not even show up and hurt you until you are 30 days past due so there is no excuse for not making your payments on time. If you have to rob Peter to pay Paul and pull money from somewhere to make a $30 payment, please do it and make your damned payments on time!

Typical Terms for Revolving Credit Lines/Cards
- 0% interest for 9 to 15 months (depending on each lender), after rates of 7 to 21% the 2nd year.
- Affordable monthly payments of just 1-2% of the balance you use, so a 10k balance has a $200 monthly payment.
- Cash access via check, cashier's check and bank wire.
- These credit lines will be with you for the life of your business and if you take care of them well, the credit limits will be increased over time.
- No Income verification or collateral is required.

0% Revolving Credit Lines/Cards
There are of course a multitude of business and personal credit lines/cards accounts that are not at 0%, and of course as an intelligent financial operator you must secure the 0% credit lines/cards accounts as it is so extremely helpful to operate with that 0% rate for the first 9 to 15 months depending on the lender.

Business Credit Lines/Cards

If you are a startup and also if your business lacks 2 years of profitable business tax returns and monthly deposits in your bank account of at least $10,000 then the only funding you can actually secure in the name of your business is business credit lines/cards. So for every new business and every existing business regardless of your financials, you will never regret having business credit lines/cards. Perhaps one of the biggest reasons is that most business credit card accounts do not report to personal credit so that means if you max them out then there will not be an adverse affect to your credit. So securing business credit lines/cards is a most for every entrepreneur who wants flexibility. Additionally if you get the right accounts you can build up miles to cover your business travel for free!

Understanding Which Lenders Pull From Which Credit Bureaus
Mortgage lenders often will pull a tri-merge credit report which is all 3 credit bureaus, Experian, Equifax and Transunion pulled at once. Most unsecured term loan lenders, traditional lines of credit lenders and revolving credit lines/cards lenders will usually pull a single or sometimes a double credit bureau pull. That's important to understand because unsecured lending is more sensitive to credit inquiries so if you go and apply at 4 lenders at once and they all pull from Experian, then after the 2nd app is submitted you are going to get some denials. That is why it is essential to go to lenders that pull from different credit bureaus as much as possible. This is why working with a funding company or acquiring the full Business Funding Formula is so vital to success when it comes to funding.

Where do you Get Revolving Credit Lines?
There are several national and regional lenders that offer business and personal credit lines/cards at 0%, so just to give you an idea of one
© The Business Funding Formula 2017

such lender, try out Capital One. The Capital One Venture card has a 0% option and also builds up tremendous travel points to fly you and your family for free as you use it to cover your expenses. For business credit lines cards Capital One offers the Capital One Spark which is a business account that also begins at 0% as well.

Access up to 90% of your Credit Lines/Cards in cash.
There are some specialized strategies to access up to 90% of the cash off of your credit lines/cards, click on either of the links below to gain access to those proprietary techniques.

To find out how much funding you can qualify for, go to www.LeoKanell.com and we will tell you within 24 hours what your Custom Funding Plan might look like for free.

Chapter 12: Not ROI, but ROL

We Know What ROI is
In the world of investing there is a term that we seem to hear more and more today and that is ROi (return on investment). So the concept goes that if you invest or put money into something, that there should be an adequate return to justify the investment in the first place. My apologies if I'm boring you, but we need to establish this definition to move on to ROL. Say I invest $1,000 in marketing, I would hope to bring in 4 or 5 times that amount to justify the marketing expense. If

you are dealing with long term investment gains then you might target a 10% return on a mutual fund, stock or real estate investment. ROI is certainly useful when determining if it makes sense to spend money or invest money into a business, project, investment or marketing campaign. Now let's take a look at how this concept applies to ROL.

ROL is a new term
So in much the same way ROI (return on investment) works for deciding when to spend money on projects and campaigns for your business or long term investments, so does the term ROL (return on loan/line) work for deciding when to accept business financing. Utilizing ROL comes down to deciding whether to take a loan, credit line or line of credit for your business. Essentially, can you generate a strong enough return on the funding in order to pay back your loan/line, cover any interest cost and net a profit for yourself and your business? If the answer is yes, then you move forward, if it is no, then you walk away. Again it is vital to understand the difference between personal and business debt and how they function. You might be thinking haven't I pounded home this point enough? The answer is unequivocally no and here's why, I have had some clients go through our funding at Leo Kanell or work through the business funding formula and had to continuously remind them that even though they are accepting a 15% rate on some business funding they are going to generate 300% on the money with the new sales the funding will generate for their business. Keep in mind, if you qualify for top tier unsecured term loans, you can secure rates from 6 to 9% and similar rates for traditional lines of credit, not to mention 0% for 9 to 15 months on select business/personal credit lines/cards. Just for the sake of example, let's dive into some examples of what good ROL metrics look like even with less than favorable terms.

© The Business Funding Formula 2017

Good ROL Metrics

Here's the first example:
- I take $50,000 in 4 revolving credit lines.
- What if I make $100,000 off of the $50k over 12 months?
- Then I will have doubled my 50k and turned it into 100k and after the 50k payback I net 50k which is a 100% return on the credit lines.

Typically these 4 credit lines might have been business/personal revolving credit lines/cards and would have been at 0% if you follow our revolving credit lines strategy described in the previous chapter 11. However, let's say that for whatever reason the 50k cost a whopping 25%, now how does the math work out?
- 50k costs me 25% simple interest over 12 months for $12,500 in interest.
- So I pay back 50k plus 12.5k interest, did I win?
- $100k (new sales) - 50k loan/lines - 12.5k interest = $37,500.

So did we win? Netting $37,500 from 50k in funding for most businesses will be a winning formula. However, to be completely objective if you have high overhead costs such as payroll, office lease, marketing and other expenses then some of those costs might eat into profits. On the other hand, you were given 50k to invest in those exact things and for most businesses $1 invested in a marketing campaign can often make 3 or 4 times more than the initial investment, let's look at another example that is more complicated.

Let's say all of your research and experience shows that you can buy inventory for your ebay business and sell it for 3 times more than you bought it at wholesale price. Very simply, if you spend $1 on inventory you sell it for $3. So back to the last example, let's say you take $50k and buy $50k worth of inventory of products that you are selling on ebay and amazon. How does this example work out?

- $50,000 in inventory purchased and sold on ebay and Amazon generates 3 times more than you actually paid for it. So you generate $150,000 in new sales (remember you can sell each unit for 3x what you pay for it,) and income for your business over 12 months.
- So at 25% interest you pay back the $50k plus 25% interest which is $12.5k over 1 year.
- Next let's say that you have additional expenses in staff, marketing and an office of $30k.
- So $150k new sales - $50k loan pay back - $12.5k interest - 30k work costs = $57,500 net profit.

Keep in mind that this example assumes you have started a new business, but if your business was somewhat established and already doing sales and running along before the funding was acquired, then this example most likely overestimates what your direct costs would be to pay employees, market and have office space. Even then, for your product and business to serve the specific increase in business due to your funding you are still netting a healthy profit. Bottom line you net an extra $57k in profits that you would not have made without the funding and you still did well even with a higher cost of capital like 25% on this particular funding. These are the types of calculations that you must do continuously with every dollar that you spend on your funding whether that is marketing, hiring staff, getting a bigger office and any investment into your business. The most successful businesses are able to find ways to generate 4 to 5 times the amount of sales from new marketing campaigns, inventory purchase and so forth.

© The Business Funding Formula 2017

If the ROL Makes Sense, Accept the Funding

Having run a few businesses and witnessed the growth of other successful businesses run by my clients over the years, I've noted what percentage a business should generate on funding to justify the acquisition of the funding in the first place. The minimum percent you should be generating at worst is a 100% return on any funding capital that you invest into your business and in reality it should be closer to 300% so that you have some wiggle room in case something goes wrong.

Imagine you get sick or the inventory you buy has some issues or you do a direct mail campaign to Florida and the week the mail is delivered there is a terrible hurricane that makes your entire direct mail investment a waste of money (that happened to me once). Although I did get one deal out of it to get my initial investment back, thanks be to that postman. If your business calculations show you that you may not generate at least a 100% return on the money then at that point it is time to revamp your business or even change businesses. All businesses are unique in the margins that they command. Even with tighter margins of 20 to 25% (meaning that from each dollar that flows into your business you have 20 to 25 cents left over) a 100% return on the money you spend on your product, service, marketing, employees or campaign, should be generating sufficient revenue from the money to net a decent profit. That is the purpose of your business.

The only other item to factor in with regard to funding is you need to add in the cost of the money (interest) and the payback of the money. Clearly with credit lines, term loans, traditional lines of credit and really most funding products there is often a payback of 3 to 5 years, not 12 months as I have shown in these examples, which gives you even more time to generate sales and revenues from your funding that you invest into your business.

Focus on Generating Revenues

At this point this is usually where my funding team has been taught to instruct the client to stop stressing out about the funding fees, interest and the funding and to turn 99% of the entrepreneur's attention to where it should be, which is income generation. You must generate sales and revenues at levels high enough to cover your costs and at quantities large enough to grow your business. Some of those previous words have been ingrained into me from one of my mentors Grant Cardone and he is certainly correct. Too often as business owners we focus our time, energies and efforts on the wrong things. At the end of the day the top priority is to grow your top number, your daily, weekly, monthly and annual sales/revenues. Businesses that think that they can grow and reap profits by continuously focusing on cutting costs will inevitably fail. So let go of the stress and become obsessed with generating new sales and revenues, if you do that, the rest of your business will fall into place.

To find out how much funding you can qualify for, go to www.LeoKanell.com and we will tell you within 24 hours what your Custom Funding Plan might look like for free.

CHAPTER 13: HUMBLE, NOT ENTITLED

Impossible Expectations

If you approach your business and funding with an attitude of deserving a 4% rate on a 100k traditional bank line of credit, as I've covered in recent chapters unless you have 2 years of very profitable business tax returns, it's not going to happen. I say this more for those searching for Startup Funding than for those business owners that are more established and understand how difficult it is to secure good business funding. There is what you want and what you will qualify for, most experienced business owners realize how difficult getting money for their business is and will be grateful for the money they secure as long as they can generate a strong return on the money. The Business Funding Formula steps will guide you to the best funding possible for your business. After that it's up to you to generate sales.

The Difference Between Secured & Unsecured

I know I have discussed this topic ad nauseum in this book, however it is worth repeating again to drive home the difference between secured and unsecured funding. Secured funding is any type of loan or line of credit that has security or collateral like real estate, stocks, bonds, your 401k, cash, equipment, vehicles and any other tangible asset that has intrinsic value that can easily be taken and sold by the lender to recoup losses for loan defaults. Secured loans especially those that are personal in nature qualify for the lowest fixed interest rates around.

Unsecured funding is every loan, credit line and line of credit that is not secured or backed by collateral and due to the increased risk for the lender will logically have higher interest rates. Again for most entrepreneurs this is going to be the funding most likely available to you unless you have hard assets that can be used as collateral.

Stay Humble

So much of life as an entrepreneur is managed by how you approach things, being unreasonably optimistic is one of those things that you must do in order to experience incredible success. Funding is no different, those that focus on problems and challenges instead of solutions will not prevail. I have seen it over and over with my clients over the years, those that have an optimistic, grateful outlook on life and the incredible opportunities we have here in America take the best funding they can get and succeed. Those that are entitled whiners will struggle for success, instead choosing to focus on a loan or rate that they believe is just too high and failing to focus completely on generating sales and revenues to build their business. Choose right now that you will take a more humble, grateful approach to funding and to your business and your odds for success will increase. The funny thing is I've been on both sides and it has always been so clear that challenges and problems will always be with us, but our ability to focus on solutions and be positive will lead to overwhelming success.

Find the Best Funding You Can Qualify For

Follow the business funding formula step by step and secure the very best funding that you can qualify for and then make that capital work for you. One of our younger clients Christian was starting a new business, he had thinner credit because he was in his early 20's, but he had the right attitude. He ended up qualifying and securing $20,000 in funding for which he was extremely grateful and immediately went to work building his business. Sure, he was hoping for more, maybe 30k to 35k, but he was not going to let anything stop him from building his own successful business and getting his piece of the american dream. Last I heard from him he was generating massive income for a young twenty something and on his way to success.

So many new entrepreneurs have completely irrational expectations and will say things like I need 100k and if I can't get it then it's not even worth getting started with my business. In most cases you don't need nearly as much as you think and can make smaller amounts work. The most important thing is to make sure that your business model is sound and working as you expect it to. Businesses certainly fail for lack of capital and access to funding, but more fail due to failing to generate sales for their business at high enough numbers to cover their expenses, make a profit and grow their business.

Remember the Power of Partners

So with all that said, let's say that you have a very detailed plan to grow your business and in reality the only way to get there is with $80k and after following the funding formula you only get to 50k, what do you do now? Well you can begin to generate enough sales and income to get there organically or you can go and find another partner with good credit that you can bring into your business in order to secure the additional 30k. With the funding formula there is always another way to get where you need to go, it just requires creativity, vision and persistence.

Finding a credit partner entails making a list of friends and family, in particular those that have been known for taking risks, that are not satisfied with mediocre finances and income. I highly recommend that you put together two things to present to a credit partner a clear business plan as well as some simple financial projections to indicate how funding will be used to generate income, profits and success. From a legal perspective you can consult an attorney or simply add the partner on to the secretary of state site for the state where your business is registered and then go and secure capital with your partner. Make it happen!

To find out how much funding you can qualify for, go to www.LeoKanell.com and we will tell you within 24 hours what your Custom Funding Plan might look like for free.

CHAPTER 14: MERCHANT CASH ADVANCE LOANS

What is a Merchant Cash Advance?
When you google business loans, often the top lending results are the so called merchant cash advance, daily payment/ach short term business loans. With the major banks and SBA pulling back their lending to small businesses significantly during the recession years of 2008 to 2009, a new business loan product took off to fill that void and gap. Some of these MCA lenders have brought value and solutions to business owners, but in my opinion many of them have put business

owners in a tough situation and in some cases even put these entrepreneurs out of business due to the very expensive nature of these loans.

WHAT ARE THESE LOANS? They are often referred to as merchant cash advances and even called lines of credit when in reality they are typically not much like that. So here's how they work, they are based off of your business bank statements as well as your credit card processing statements. so let's say that you run $25,000 on average through your merchant processing and/or your business bank statements and even if you have less than perfect credit you can often qualify for a short term cash advance that is based on your future sales. Generally these loans are very short term in nature and these loans are paid back by the lender withdrawing a daily payment out of your business bank account. That's right I said daily payment so monday thru friday there is a withdrawal hitting your bank account.

What are Typical MCA terms?
What are typical terms? The typical terms for these short term loans are usually 3-10 month terms, loan amounts are calculated based off of your average monthly business bank deposits, so if you do 25k on average in monthly deposits then that will often allow you to get a loan amount equal to your monthly business bank deposits on average. So you basically have 3-12 months to pay back the loan and these lenders will often say that you are not paying an interest rate, but rather a payment rate, typical payment rates are 1.25 to 145, meaning that you pay 25 cents to 45 cents on each dollar. Damn, that's expensive for a 6 month loan!

Common loan terms are 6 to 8 month terms, here's a typical loan term: $25,000 loan, 8 month term to pay it all back, with daily payments coming out of your bank account Monday-Friday, you will pay back $35,000 for the $25,000. (about 40% paid back over 8 months. Daily payments of about $200 Monday-Friday, so in this example you'd pay back $1,000 per week and $4,000 per month in order to pay it back in a little over 8 months. To the public these loans may seem like loan sharking and even appear to be illegal. Rest assured they are absolutely legal, and in some cases they do make sense, but certainly not many, let's look at how you qualify. Payment rate is the key phrase in MCA loans and is also the term that business owners are most confused by.

How do you qualify?

Credit score is not overly important and can legitimately go down to a 550, it is important that the past 2 year history be somewhat decent, no big charge offs, collections or judgments. Bk's, tax liens and other items do not disqualify a client. Dirty personal credit will lead to shorter term loans however. The big key with these loans is how you care for your business bank statement, they are looking for 2 things, that you carry a decent daily average balance in your biz bank account and that you also avoid NSF charges for having insufficient funds to cover payments and they don't want to see negative bank balance days. Most lenders will not allow more than 3 to 4 negative days over a 3 month period or more than 4 or 5 NSF's, if they do of course the rate will be higher, and the loan term shorter.

So if you take care of your business bank account, have personal credit that isn't too terrible and have been in business for at least 2-3 years then you can often get a loan from these daily payment lenders.

© The Business Funding Formula 2017

They will often advertise that if you've been in business for a year, then they will lend to you, but that is very rare indeed. They also have lots of business types that are restricted or that they do not lend to because of high default rates Some of the high risk businesses they do not lend to are: accountants, attorneys (odd isn't it?) car sales, finance companies, employment agencies, mlms, gambling, insurance, real estate, religious and travel agencies. Restricted industries are often: trucking, transportation, tv, marketing, home health, it, grocery stores, builders and home based businesses. They love to lend to Doctors, dentists, liquor stores, restaurants, auto repair, tire shops, home health care and other seemingly low risk industries.

MCA and Expensive Lenders to Avoid
Yellowstone Capital out of New York and LoanMe out of California are probably the two most expensive lenders in this category. Yellowstone typically offers a 2 or 3 month loan at an astounding high interest rate of 35 to 50% over 90 days which if there were an effective APR would put it in the 140%+ range. LoanMe is not necessarily a merchant cash advance company, but they offer loans with typical rates of 69% to 120%. As I have explained in previous chapters there are situations where if you know your business and your ROL is sufficiently high then you will certainly still net a profit with a loan this expensive. However why should you when there are certainly better funding options available than what either of these companies offers. There are enough legit MCA companies available that offer longer terms of 9 to 15 months and pay back rates that are much less.

How do you Find good Merchant Cash Advance Lenders?
There are so many merchant cash advance lenders out there, one of the biggest and oldest is Can Capital: (www.CanCapital.com) these

guys are the originals, they do a nice job, offer longer term loans and have also introduced some additional term loans. I find that their rates are generally more affordable, they are a solid lender for MCA/daily payment loans. Turn around times are quick and they can often fund you within a week or two or even sooner in some cases.

If you don't qualify for an sba loan or the other business term loans, then honestly I would go for the unsecured term loans or unsecured credit lines before ever considering a daily payment loan. That said, I have gotten a daily payment loan before for one of my businesses and it can come in handy once in awhile, let's talk about when it makes the most sense to take out a daily payment loan. Your business should be growing, you should be confident in future sales and also be in a business that can make a quick, strong return on the loan. Some examples are often businesses like restaurants or construction businesses that can buy inventory or parts and make a return of 3 or 4 times the cost of the inventory. For businesses like that it can make sense indeed.

To find out how much funding you can qualify for, go to www.LeoKanell.com and we will tell you within 24 hours what your Custom Funding Plan might look like for free.

CHAPTER 15: SBA FOR ESTABLISHED BUSINESSES

How SBA Works

SBA can guarantee as much as 85 percent on loans of up to $150,000 and 75 percent on loans of more than $150,000. SBA's maximum exposure amount is $3,750,000. Thus, if a business receives an SBA-guaranteed loan for $5 million, the maximum guarantee to the lender will be $3,750,000 or 75%. SBA Express loans have a maximum guarantee set at 50 percent.

For that reason and due to the fact that many banks lost significantly on business loans that defaulted during the recession, the majority of all bank financing is nearly always an SBA loan since the risk is so much less for them. That means if they are holding the bag on a loan that they the bank fund themselves, they are likely to be even more stringent in a lot of cases than they will be with an SBA loan. SBA loans are never gotten straight from the SBA, they are funded from banks.

Profitable Business Tax Returns are Key

When it comes to SBA loans and bank loans, the top qualifying factor that sets apart businesses with a solid chance of qualifying for money and those businesses that have no shot at qualifying for an SBA loan is profitable business tax returns. Before we dive in let's look at how SBA and bank financing works. Most banks prefer to make SBA loans, they limit the bank's risk significantly since the Small Business Administration will help to cover the risk of a loan that defaults.

The Tricks of Business Tax Return Income

Business net Income: The highest hurdle for a business to qualify for any type of SBA loan begins with showing net income on a business tax return. For an SBA loan to be funded the lender and the SBA will calculate the debt service ratio and global ratio for the business and its owner personally. The reality is that most small businesses will end up showing a loss or break even business tax return which means that for most business owners it is difficult to qualify for an SBA loan. That said there are of course businesses that do qualify so let's break down this hurdle and how it's calculated.

Business net income is calculated by adding in owner/officer compensation like salaries and payments paid to the owner that are actual income to the owner. You can also add in depreciation, interest, amortization and of course the ordinary business net income that is shown at the bottom of each business tax return. When you add all of those numbers up they need to be high enough to cover the new payments from a new business loan and still leave a buffer. They also need to be high enough to cover the personal expenses of the business owner (s) and the new business loan payment and still leave a decent buffer each month.

So let's look at an example, let's say you paid yourself as the owner of your business a salary (w2) of $50,000 that shows on pg 1 of the business tax return as owner compensation, officer compensation, payments to owner etc. Then you have $20,000 in interest payments and $10,000 in depreciation. Amortization is only calculated if you pay on a commercial mortgage, in this case you don't have one so that number is 0. Your business net income is $5,000, hey you wrote off your expenses like most owners, but you may still qualify, here's how. So 50k owner/officer compensation, plus 20k interest, plus 10k depreciation and 5k business net income is a total of $85,000. Let's say that your new SBA loan payments are $2,500 per month x 12 months which is $30,000, so $85k is obviously big enough to cover the 30k, good. Next all of your personal expenses on credit add up to $35,000 annually which leaves a buffer of about $20,000, $85,000-$30,000 (new biz loan annual payments) - $35,000 (personal expenses on credit) = $20,000. $20k in buffer is probably enough for many lenders, but it will depend on the lender.

2 years of profitable business tax returns and personal income tax returns showing enough income to cover your personal expenses are minimum requirements for most sba loans, however in many cases 3 years of profitable business tax returns may be required.
Let's look at additional requirements: 2 years in business, for profit business, non-profits don't qualify. Individuals owning 20% of business cannot work for SBA or have criminal background, and must be legal permanent resident or us citizen. Personal credit score of at least 600, but most often a 640 is what most banks require and the majority of funding takes place at a 680 credit score. No Bankruptcy, foreclosure, judgments or tax liens in the last 3 years. No charge offs or open collections are allowed. They will also check your business credit, the quickest, most affordable method to do that is by going to www.nav.com and getting your D&B, Fico and Experian Business
© The Business Funding Formula 2017

reports. If your report is very weak, and you are dead set on securing an sba loan then I recommend you focus on the Business credit building portion of the business funding formula, realize it will take a few months to build your business credit, but you may get declined if you have negative or no business credit established.

FINDING AN SBA LENDER:

Assets & collateral that is acceptable see:
https://www.sba.gov/content/collateral

This isn't rocket science, you need to work with an SBA lender who is at least in the top 100 and located close to where you live. Here is the list of the top 100 SBA lenders updated. https://www.sba.gov/lenders-top-100

•Here's a good link to get connected to a local SBA lender
•https://www.sba.gov/tools/linc Keep in mind it can be like going down a rabbit hole. Do not allow any personal credit hard pulls until you are pre-approved.

SBA ineligible Businesses are Listed Below:

- •Here is the full list: https://www.sba.gov/content/7a-loan-program-eligibility
- •Financial: lending, banks, finance companies, loan brokers etc.
- •Real Estate (all types,) insurance, gambling, private memberships.
- •Instructing, counseling, consulting, religion.
- •Sexual businesses, political.

© The Business Funding Formula 2017

- •Oil & other speculative businesses

SBA Programs Include 7(a), 504 & Express

Let's take a look at the 3 types of SBA Loans in this chart:

Small Business Administration (SBA) Financing Table

Loan Type	SBA 504	SBA 7(A) Loans	SBA Express
Use it for	Purchase equipment or real estate (no refinancing) Construction and renovation	Purchase or expand a business Purchase equipment or inventory Working capital Refinance debt	Working capital Purchase equipment Purchase vehicles or inventory
Benefits	Longer maturity than conventional loan Lower down payments on fixed assets Easier qualification than a conventional loan	Longer maturity than conventional loan Lower down payments on fixed assets Easier qualification than a conventional loan	Longer maturity than some conventional loans Easier qualification than a conventional loan
Amount	$350,000 minimum, no maximum	$350,000- $5,000,000	$25,000-$350,000
Terms	Up to 2 years	Up to 7 years for working	7-year term with

© The Business Funding Formula 2017

	interim construction period 7-10 years on equipment 10-20 years on real estate	capital Up to 10 years for equipment or business acquisition Up to 25 years for real estate	first-year revolving option and balance amortized across the remainder of the term

The bottom line is that in order to qualify for the SBA 504 or SBA 7(A) Loans your business will need to have significantly profitable tax returns in order to qualify for an SBA loan as well as provide tremendous collateral that is worth more than the loan that you request. For example, let's say you need a piece of equipment for $500,000, the value of the equipment should be worth more than the loan amount. In most cases a down payment of at least 10% is required and in many cases a down payment of up to 25% is often required for larger loans.

So collateral and down payment are things that you must have for the larger loan amounts offered through the 504 and 7a. The 504 is for equipment and real estate only while the 7a can be used for working capital, but will still require inventory and equipment to cover as collateral for the loan.

For the majority of small businesses, the SBA express loan with amounts from $25k to $350k will be the best option for most business owners, that said there are lots of banks that claim to do sba loans and that said it is difficult to ascertain what banks you can trust, but the list of the top 100 is pretty clear and one of those banks should be in your local area.

© The Business Funding Formula 2017

Smaller Loans Do Not Need Collateral

The other cool factor about the sba express is it is the one sba loan that doesn't require collateral and assets to back it up, you can literally secure a $150,000 loan completely unsecured based on having 2 to 3 years of profitable business tax returns. Rate is generally 6-7% paid back over 10 years, so the payment is very low and affordable. For loans above $150k to $350k some form of equipment or commercial real estate will be needed as collateral.

Typical SBA Terms

Some of the typical terms that SBA will give out include much longer terms of 7 to 10 years for working capital type loans. For secured loans involving real estate and equipment there are even longer terms up to 25 years. Secured SBA loans like the 504 or 7a come with very low rates as low as in the 4 to 5% range which is amazing. For the SBA express and other working capital loans under 150k rates are typically around 6 to 8%. If you go down the SBA road, go with patience because it can be a long process.

To find out how much funding you can qualify for, go to www.LeoKanell.com and we will tell you within 24 hours what your Custom Funding Plan might look like for free.

CHAPTER 16: TERM LOANS & LINES OF CREDIT FOR ESTABLISHED BUSINESSES

Alternatives to SBA Financing

An Alternative that's quicker and nearly as good as SBA with a much higher rate of approvals. So while SBA loans can take several weeks and have significant document requirements, there is another option that comes with nearly the same low interest rates and benefits of an SBA loan. While SBA will always require collateral and assets in order to secure funding above $150,000, there are several business term loan lenders who will lend much higher than $150k and still not require any type of collateral. So let's take a look at the top ones now.

How to Qualify

Though these loans get done at a higher percentage than SBA loans, there are still a lot of turndowns when it comes to these solid biz term loans, it is also possible that they may not like your specific line of business if they find you to be a higher risk. The qualifying criteria is generally very similar with most business term lenders, they will want to see at least 2 years of profitable business tax returns, 2 years of personal tax returns showing enough income to cover you personal expenses, YTD Profit & Loss & Balance Sheet aka business financials, they will want a first lien position typically. If you have a good SBA loan already, then they may consider taking a 2nd lien position with your business. UCC liens are filed with the secretary of state where your business is registered and acts similarly to a title company that registers a first mortgage lien on a real estate property like your primary residence.

They will also want to see a list of your current loans against your business and positive business credit history. They want to see very little existing business debt on the business and of course they will verify your identity with a driver's license and other items.

Typical Terms

Terms are typically 2 to 5 year terms and rates are usually from 7 to 20%. So the rates are higher and the terms a not as long which means that your monthly payments will be higher than an sba loan, but paying off your business debt sooner is not necessarily a bad thing.

Pros & Cons vs SBA

The obvious pros with an SBA loan are that the rates are typically lower and the terms are longer which means that your monthly payments are lower, however the biggest problem with SBA is that you are declined more often than at these alternative lenders. The other issue is that SBA does take a long time, I don't' care who you talk to at your local bank or what person tells you that your SBA loan can close within a couple of weeks, having worked in the trenches on multi million dollar and smaller SBA loans, they have always taken months of time, mountains of paperwork and then after all of that they can still be declined. Perhaps one of the reasons why is that you are dealing with a government entity in the SBA and even though the loans are issued from banks, the SBA still has to give their stamped seal of approval on the loan and that can take time and also lead to uncertainty.

Most business owners and entrepreneurs that I have worked with value correctly their time above all else, so that being the case the biggest pros with these alternative term loans for established businesses are that the time constraints are lower.

Funding Circle, An Excellent Alternative Business Term Lender
They offer 1-5 year term loans from $25,000 to $500,000, they are in my opinion the leader when it comes to solid term loans and provide many benefits when compared with SBA. Their rates range from 6% to 20%, and with a term of 4-5 years that is a very affordable monthly payment.

The biggest differences between SBA and Funding Circle is that FC is faster, requires less paperwork and will offer loan amounts above 150k all the way to 500k without requiring collateral. Their customer service is excellent, and they are experienced, in the UK they have funded a lot of business and globally they have already funded over 1.5B in business loans, an incredible accomplishment. I have personally run clients through them with great success. Clean Public Records on your personal credit is critical since they are selling these loans on an open market.
© The Business Funding Formula 2017

Simply go to www.FundingCircle.com and make sure you see the US flag to the upper right corner and submit an app. FC prefers to lend to businesses with 3 years of profitable business tax returns, however one year can be break even or non profitable. Unlike SBA they will not lend to any business owner with any type of public record like a bk, tax lien, judgment etc. They also have 0 tolerance for business tax liens and business credit issues. Remember they are selling the loan to investors who want to invest in a good business loan. If you have cash in the bank or an IRA or retirement account that can go a long way to making them comfortable to lend to you. They will hard pull your credit with Experian as will most sba lenders.

Make your case to your underwriter, if you pass the initial qualifications which will be of course enough business profits to cover a new business loan, the same calculations as SBA apply for income. You can add in owner income, interest, amortization, depreciation and biz net income and as long as there is enough to cover your personal expenses and your new business loan and you have a buffer, then you stand a good chance of getting approved. After that then you will have a big call with a FC underwriter, this is your chance to show your passion about your business.. You must however, back it up with cold, hard numbers of your future growth of your business and why. Cash in the biz account is king or some type of IRA will make them feel much more comfortable.

The Unicorn (Business line of credit)

The traditional business line of credit is perhaps the most sought after product in business funding and for good reason. Business lines of credit unlike the traditional lines of credit covered in chapter 10 are in the name of the business and typically come with lower long term rates when compared to business credit lines/cards. They are in the name of your business and do not report to personal credit. Additionally it is more convenient to access the cash off of these business lines of credit when compared to the multiple step process of liquidating cash off of a credit line/card type account. Like the previously covered business term loans in this chapter, qualifying for a business line of credit is very similar.

How to Qualify

In order to qualify for a business line of credit you will need at least 2 and if you have 3 years worth of profitable business tax returns and financials that will be very helpful to secure a traditional business line of credit. A lower debt to income ratio will be required including adequate cash flow from your business to continue to pay your business bills, personal bills and have excess cash leftover to cover the payments on your business line of credit. The more profitable your business and the higher your annual sales and revenue, the larger your business line of credit will be. Typically a line of credit up to $100k can be unsecured without collateral, but anything over 100k seems to be the spot where most lenders will want to have the security of equipment, equity in real estate, inventory and any other easily sold assets to be able to secure a larger business line of credit. A significant difference between business lines of credit and business term loans is that lenders are much more stringent with your business and personal credit. They really want to see a 720 or better personal credit score and a high business credit score with Dun & Bradstreet, Experian and Equifax Business. They also want to see lower credit utilization rates with any existing lines of credit you have personally.

© The Business Funding Formula 2017

Where to find Business Lines of Credit

Business lines of credit are found with the nation's largest banks and lenders, probably the 2 banks at the top of the list are US Bank and Wells Fargo, each have a strong focus on helping businesses secure funding. Each will require as will other major banks that you establish your business banking accounts with them in order to apply for a business line of credit. One of the misnomers about business lines of credit is this idea that they will be as cheap and affordable as a personal line of credit, and that is simply not the case, remember business and especially if it is unsecured will require higher rates. Rates may be from 7 to 12% and because they are lines of credit and the lender doesn't' know when you will use them, the rates are always variable and will almost never be fixed. Payback can be flexible, but most banks and lenders will require that if the line is not paid back within 2 years of carrying a balance, then they will set up a fixed pay back of the entire limit. Many lenders seem to be requiring that these lines are typically paid back within 2 years.

An online lender who has done a nice job of putting together a solid business line of credit product is www.Kabbage.com , they have a flexible line of credit for your business and in the name of the business, it must be paid back within 12 months and the rates will be higher than a typical bank, but they are excellent to work with and the line of credit is truly flexible and can be accessed any time. They also will not ask for business tax returns, but instead look at upward trending bank deposits and verification of other business accounts like your merchant account and google adwords marketing account as proof of a growing business.

To find out how much funding you can qualify for, go to www.LeoKanell.com and we will tell you within 24 hours what your Custom Funding Plan might look like for free.

CHAPTER 17: BUSINESS CREDIT & HOW IT WORKS

What is Business Credit

The majority of business owners according to Dun & Bradstreet don't know that their business has a business credit profile and score.

Regardless of whether your business is new or established, establishing your business credit will lay a strong foundation that will help your business for years to come. The purpose of establishing business credit is so that when you apply for unsecured business credit lines, a bank loan or any type of business financing, lenders will approve you for larger funding amounts and lower interest rates because of your business credit. While it is not overly complicated, very few business owners know and understand the process of setting up business credit. We will dive into this often misunderstood tool that businesses must establish for long term success.

Why Does It Matter?

By building a strong business credit profile the enterprising business owner can then secure financing and build an incredible reputation based solely on the company's business credit. That means that it is no longer necessary for the business owner to utilize their personal credit or to personally guarantee everything connected with the business. Ask yourself does Bill Gates use his personal credit to fund his business? How about the Walton family that owns much of Walmart do they personally guarantee everything for Walmart? The answer is a resounding no because of the fact that they have shrewdly developed an impeccable corporate credit profile and the good news is that regardless of the size of your business you can do the same. One other tidbit about corporate credit, is that it is public record, anyone can go online and pull the business credit report for any business without asking for permission. Imagine you are trying to land a big job with a big company and they check your business credit what will they find? Corporate credit matters and helps to separate personal matters from your business.

4 Reasons Why Business Credit Matters

1. *Reduce personal liability*: Avoid risking your personal credit, home & assets, put the risk on the business where it belongs.
2. *Real Corporate Credit & Funding:* Secure massive funding from your business' credit score not your personal credit score.
3. *Increase the Value of your Business:* Some day you may wish to sell your business or just have it appraised, it will be worth a lot more if it has corporate credit established.
4. *Land big contracts:* Before a government entity or large corporation decides to do business with you they will check your business credit report and a good business credit score will be the deciding factor whether they work with you.

Some clients of mine, Steve & Lennett owned a private school in Southern California, they needed to secure capital in order to recruit more students. We checked their business credit first and noticed that a previous business at their business location had erroneously been merged into their D&B report. With such a terrible business report, their business would have been denied financing everywhere automatically. So we contacted D&B and it took about a month to clear up, but it was well worth it when they secured over $200k in unsecured credit lines so they could grow their business, without it they might have been denied at most lenders. **Understanding your business credit is a vital key to securing business funding.**

Who are the Business Credit Bureaus?

© The Business Funding Formula 2017

The first thing to understand is that while personal credit is monitored by 3 bureaus which are Experian, equifax and transunion, in business it is similar they are broken down into Dun & Bradstreet, Business Experian and Equifax Business. The biggest difference is that the business credit bureaus do not report credit automatically the reason for this is that other businesses that supply business credit like your local suppliers often do not report to business credit so you may have a $20k line of credit for inventory at your local supplier, but because they do not report to the business credit bureaus, your strong history does not show up on your business report. So what you will need to do is call up each business credit bureau and in some cases they will be able to verify the payment history and report the account to help build your business credit. They will of course charge you to do it, but it'll be worth it. If they will not then you need to buy from suppliers who will report to the business credit bureaus in order to establish strong business credit.

The Business Credit Building process has 3 steps:

1. Create and establish a business credit profile with all 3 credit bureaus.
2. Ensure your credit profiles are correct and begin to secure business credit accounts that report to your business credit profiles.
3. Learn to read your reports and monitor them for accuracy and results.

© The Business Funding Formula 2017

Dun & Bradstreet (D&B)

Find out if your business has a Duns #, if it doesn't you can apply for a free Duns # and receive it in 30 days or pay $49 to get it in a week. Most importantly verify that your company information is correct with them including, address, biz phone etc. Avoid supplying financial info to them if you are new.

SET UP YOUR D&B FILE, GET A DUNS # FOR FREE with the link below.

http://www.dnb.com/get-a-duns-number.html

D&B gives you a PAYDEX SCORE from 0-100, an 80 is considered a good paydex score.

Here are some tips when applying for the free duns #. Use the correct business information. It is important that your business name, address, phone number and other business information is correct on your business credit report. The information listed on your business credit report and all other business records should be the same.

If possible the business should have an actual physical business address. An actual physical business location can add business credibility. Your business Address should be an actual address listed with the United States postal service. For example if you are using a suite number that isn't actually a listed suite with the United Postal Service your address can't be verified by lenders or the business credit agencies. Additionally don't share a business address with any other businesses to avoid reporting issues.

Be prepared to answer verification question. D & B's system will ask personal background questions to verify the business owner. This insures that an actual authorized individual sets up the business's

DUNs #. If you find you are having issues with D & B's website make sure you have updated your browser and java. If this still doesn't resolve the issues you may have to call d & b customer service to apply for your free duns #.

Business Experian

Simply search the experian business database to see if your company has a profile. Always verify that no unfavorable or incorrect info like a lien or collection or late payment are reporting.

Experian gives businesses an "INTELLISCORE" like D&B from 0-100, 75 + is good.

Make sure to apply with vendors who report to experian Business. Update your report on the experian business link below.

http://www.experian.com/small-business/business-credit-information.jsp

Equifax Business

Your Business Equifax report is created as creditors or vendors report payment history onto your business credit reports. You will use the search engine for Equifax to see if your business currently has a business credit report with Equifax. The search engine will bring up the business names that are the closest match to your corporation. If your company isn't listed that simply means that you need to establish credit with lenders or trade accounts that report to Business Equifax.

How do you start the process?

© The Business Funding Formula 2017

https://sb.econsumer.equifax.com/bizdirect/smallBusinessSearch.ehtml

- Apply for credit with creditors that report to business Equifax.

Building Business Credit

Keep in mind that most business creditors do check business credit but most don't report payment history back to the business credit bureaus. Even when a creditor does report to business credit it doesn't mean that they report to all 3 business credit agencies. It is important to verify your business credit account reports before applying.

- Make a purchase

When making your purchase make sure you use your new business credit account. If you pay too soon the credit terms aren't utilized.

- Make a payment

Once you have made a purchase wait for your invoice or bill to be generated. It is this payment that is reported to the business credit bureau.

Your payments should be on time or preferably early so that the creditor reports positive payment history. A late payment can damage your business credibility. It takes 30-60 days for your payment to show on your business credit report.

When you applied for your credit account it is important that you used the correct business information including business name, address & payment data. It is these details that get reported to the business credit agency.

© The Business Funding Formula 2017

Some vendors you can get established with to begin building your corporate credit are: Quill.com, you can buy office supplies, Gemplers.com you can buy outdoor work supplies, Ulline.com you can buy cleaning materials, and at Grainger.com you can buy additional equipment for your business. Remember to apply for business credit accounts, buy something that costs at least $50 and make your payment early, within a few weeks you will establish business credit.

Monitor your reports & Learn how to Read the Reports

Let's look at www.nav.com

This is the best and most affordable way to check your business credit reports, simply go to the site and sign up for the $29 plan, you can cancel after you access your reports, it is only a month to month contract.

For $29 you will have access to a detailed D&B report, Fico SBA report and Experian Business report.

To find out how much funding you can qualify for, go to www.LeoKanell.com and we will tell you within 24 hours what your Custom Funding Plan might look like for free.

© The Business Funding Formula 2017

CHAPTER 18: PUTTING IT ALL TOGETHER & FUNDING FOLLOW UP

Congratulations on making it to this point, since we have now completed all facets of the business funding formula, it definitely seems appropriate to review the funding formula steps one more time and make sure that the funding formula is clear.

Funding = Steps 1 through 10 of the Business Funding Formula.

STEP 1: Are you a Startup or Established Business
STEP 2: Assess your Credit & Income
STEP 3: SBA & Secured Funding First
STEP 4: Look at Unsecured Term Loans
STEP 5: Traditional Lines of Credit
STEP 6: Revolving Credit Lines/Cards
STEP 7: SBA for Established Businesses
STEP 8: Term Loans & Lines of Credit for Established Businesses (non SBA)
STEP 9: Corporate Credit Development
STEP 10: Putting it all Together and Funding Follow up
STEP 11: Funding Rules to Live By

© The Business Funding Formula 2017

Funding Combinations

As you go through the funding steps I have found it helpful to put together funding combinations to ensure that you absolutely reap the best funding results possible. For example, if you are a newer startup I believe a good combination is to secure a term loan perhaps to pay down credit card balances or just for quick cash. After your term loan funds, pay down your high balance credit cards, then verify via your CreditCheckTotal.com account that updates daily that each new, lower balance is reporting. Next secure 1 to 2 traditional lines of credit and then 4 or 5 revolving credit lines/cards at 0%. Top it all off with some corporate credit development so that in the future you can qualify for either an SBA or established business term loan or business line of credit. Any kind of funding involving a partner you bring into the business will follow this same formula as well.

So the Funding Formula for Startup Funding = 1+2+4+5+6+9+10+11

If you are an established business without profitable business tax returns then you would follow a very similar if not exact funding process as presented in the previous paragraph, but if your business does have 2 years of profitable business tax returns then you might acquire an sba loan, business term loan or business line of credit and then still secure business credit lines/cards at 0% and then afterwards keep building your business credit profile.

The Funding Formula for Established might be = 1+2+7+8+6+9+11

Funding combinations like those presented here will give you great flexibility and funding power to be able to take your

© The Business Funding Formula 2017

business to the next level or the all important first level if your business is new.

The FUNDING is in the Follow Up

One of the common mistakes that a lot of people make is that after they apply for their funding they then wait for the lender to get in touch with them and update them on the status of their loans, credit lines/cards and funding applications. This is a mistake, when you follow up quickly you show the lender this is a priority, if you don't then your application may sit there and not be approved due to not following up in a timely manner. Lenders are concerned with identity theft and so if you do not follow up with a funding application they may just decline you based on no communication. Of course with any of the applications in which the lender automatically approved you for funding you may not need to contact them, it is common sometimes for a lender to approve you and not disclose or tell you for how much you were approved. So if that happens to you with any lender, be sure to call the lender that approved you, but didn't tell you for how much so you know how much you were approved for and confirm the details.

Over and over it has been proven to be most effective to contact each lender within 24 to 48 hours. With every pending credit application make a concerted effort to contact each lender quickly. By following up quickly there is no question for the lender that you want the credit line or loan and that you are the real person who applied which allows the lender to verify your identity over the phone which increases the odds for the bank you will be a good client.

Your Attitude Does Matter

© The Business Funding Formula 2017

When you call the lender, realize that your attitude can make a difference, if you are positive and confident about yourself, your income, and your business you will significantly increase the odds that you can convince an underwriter to approve you for larger credit lines and approvals instead of deny you. I will say that with credit line/card type accounts it can make a really big difference. Be sure to tell the lenders things that make sense, for example if you have an existing 10k card in your personal name and then apply for a business credit card, it may be helpful to tell the business lender that you are looking for an identical 10k limit account in the name of your business so you can stop using a personal card for business purposes. These types of real explanations go far with underwriters. Anytime you can build a case about why you personally or your business are a good bet you need to do this. The underwriters and decision makers at each lender are people at the end of the day, if you treat them right and plead your case including that you have great credit, income and are very responsible, then they will be more likely to approve you or even to overturn a denial. Obviously that doesn't always happen, but it certainly can.

What if You are Declined

I remember one client emailing me that she had been declined by a lender for a credit line/card account, I told her that was ridiculous and that she should optimistically and respectfully point out all of the reasons why she was a good borrower and have the lender take another look at it or as we say in lending "reconsider," the app. The lender did and then issued a $10,000 approval at 0% for 15 months. So this doesn't always happen, but certainly can if you follow up correctly. In some cases if you are declined initially by a lender you can explain the strong points of your credit, your business, your income and in particular your credit history. If you have multiple credit lines and credit cards and auto loans and mortgages that you have paid on time for years it is important that you point out these strong points, sometimes the lender system may flag you and decline your app, so it's imperative that you push back against the lender rep very politely, diplomatically and passionately and ask them to reconsider your application.

Verify your Identity

For most lenders whether they offer term loans, lines of credit or revolving credit lines/cards when you call the lender, typically you will need to answer some identity questions like your DOB, SSN, address, cell phone number and sometimes they will ask you specific questions about your credit in an effort to verify your identity.

Questions may go like this, "you opened a new car loan in April of 2016, what is the monthly payment amount on that account?" Whenever you are answering specific questions about your identity, it is highly important that you take your time to answer those questions correctly. Whenever you answer those questions and call those lenders make sure that you have a copy of your credit report in front of you and perhaps your budget with all of your current loans, lenders and details for those amounts. For the most part you should remember most of the answers to the questions, but if you do not then take your time answering them correctly.

In general most pending personal credit cards/lines will have approval decisions within 2-3 days. Business credit lines however can take anywhere from a few days all the way up to 2 weeks to make a decision. Larger business term and lines of credit lenders may take 2 to 3 weeks. With business credit lines often lenders will request a copy of your articles of organization for your business entity or the EIN (Tax ID) documents from the IRS, usually something to verify the address & name of your business entity.

The bottom line is to just be very proactive, positive and persistent in your funding follow up and that way you will give yourself every opportunity to secure as much funding as possible and at the very best terms. A few tips, apply online from home always, as lenders now verify your identity by matching up your internet service provider location through your IP and want it to match with where you live. In other words don't apply while on vacation in Florida if you live in Pennsylvania. Wait till you get home and then apply.

To find out how much funding you can qualify for, go to www.LeoKanell.com and we will tell you within 24 hours what your Custom Funding Plan might look like for free.

CHAPTER 19: FULL SERVICE FUNDING VS DO IT YOURSELF

Pros & Cons of Full Service Funding
So there are essentially two ways to secure funding, you can either do it yourself or utilize the services of a funding company. Let's look at the pros of a funding company. First, you are more apt to actually secure better funding since the funding company does this every day so they will have their pulse on the lending environment and have a very good idea of the best places to go to secure funding for you and your business. Additional pros are that you don't have to spend your

time (your most valuable asset) trying to figure out the right funding, what you qualify for and how to correctly fill out the funding applications. Probably the biggest positive is not having to worry about whether you are going to qualify for a certain type of funding or not. While the funding company may not be able to specifically guarantee you the funding you want, they will certainly put as many odds in your favor as possible by taking you to the right lenders in the right order.

The biggest problem with funding in general is going to the wrong lenders that end up denying you funding instead of approving you which can lead to funding failure. You only have so many inquiries that you can take on your credit before all lenders begin to deny you, because they assume with so many inquiries you either already received funding or your profile has a major issue that make you a bad funding client. Either way working with a funding company who only gets paid for successfully helping you to secure funding ensures that they are motivated to take you to the funding options most likely to actually approve you for funding.

There are of course cons working with a funding company, the top one that we all fear is actually having to pay out funding fees for the funding service. As long as you are working with a company that doesn't get paid unless they secure funding first, that way you ensure that they are 100% motivated to get the job done. The next issue or con is what if they take you to a lender that has secret fees and actually pays a kickback to the funding company which may not be the best funding that you actually qualify for, but rather the option that pays the funding company the most money. This is a real concern, so when selecting a company that secures funding for you it is best to work with a company that does not receive kickbacks of any kind so that they are motivated to objectively select the best funding that you can qualify for and not the option that pays them the biggest commission. Those are the cons to be aware of.

Where to go for Full Service Funding?
So there is a small, but growing group of funding companies that secure funding for entrepreneurs, most of them focus the majority of their time and efforts securing only merchant cash advance loans for their clients. As I discussed in chapter 14, MCA loans should really be a last resort and are often not the best funding option for a business and if you are a new business owner then they aren't even an option. The other group of funding companies focus 99% of their funding towards revolving credit lines/cards type accounts and that is it, they don't provide term loans, they don't facilitate the paying down of your maxed out credit cards so that you can qualify for traditional lines of credit or revolving credit lines. They almost never provide established business funding options either which is problematic if you have hopes of becoming an established business or obviously if you already are an established business looking for better funding options.

Another key service that a funding company should provide is access to funding education to help ensure that an entrepreneur not only secures the best funding that they can qualify for now, but also provides education so the business owner knows how to build business credit, secure sba funding for an established business and most importantly make good decisions with the funding that they acquire by way of using the funding service.

In reality I am only aware of one funding company that provides all funding types including term loans, actual lines of credit, revolving credit lines/cards, established business funding options, business credit education and long term funding education with a beautiful platform. This funding company also only earns money by securing funding for the client, in other words they are performance based and yet they don't take kickbacks from other lenders so that you can confidently know they are not just sending to the lender paying the biggest commissions and that is Leo Kanell Funding. Go to www.LeoKanell.com full disclosure as you might imagine that is indeed my funding company, I am the CEO and founder and I believe we have the very best Funding Managers, Advisers and Specialists that are completely dedicated and on a mission to guaranteeing you the very best funding that you can qualify for period.

Pros & Cons of Do It Yourself
So with all of that said, there are groups of people like never before that possess the passion and the will to learn how to do things themselves. There are of course pros to trying to secure the money yourself. Obviously you will not have to pay a funding company any fees to secure funding. The biggest cons are that you will have to spend a decent amount of time trying to ensure that you actually get yourself the very best funding possible. Not to mention trying to figure out which lenders you can qualify for and which lenders you can trust to actually do what they promise. Also the job of assessing your credit and income and understanding new terms will take some time. Would your time be better spent elsewhere, working on your business and generating sales and revenues? That is the choice that you will need to make.

Where to Find Funding Guidance to Do it yourself
There are a lot of resources around online from the SBA to business credit services and many different articles for you to read, however I

have never seen any company or individual put together as effective and efficient of a business funding process as the business funding formula and training found at www.7Figures.com, in reality I know because I looked back around October of 2015 I began to look around and see if anyone had put together a comprehensive business funding education program with the nuts and bolts and no fluff. I found nothing, there is still very little available and the business funding formula in its entirety is found at www.7Figures.com and includes specific guidance to the very best funding options including access to my rolodex of lenders for each funding category from unsecured term loans to lines of credit to revolving credit lines and the right order to apply for each funding option which makes all the difference between funding and failure. A list of all of the benefits of the full Business Funding Formula are found below:

Benefits of the Business Funding Formula
- 10 years of funding expertise guiding you to success, Saves you a ton of time!
- Real Results, Same Formula that has worked for me personally and countless clients.
- Road map to the best financing you can qualify for, no need to wonder if you're getting screwed.
- Saves you thousands on broker fees, lender fees and interest.
- Helps you avoid expensive loans that can put you out of business
- Lifetime Access to the Best Business Funding for any business type
- Includes a Plan B, C, D and so on for every funding solution, if one lender doesn't work out the next best options are right there easily accessible.

The Business Funding Formula 2017

- Most importantly, Helps you to Jumpstart your business and grow faster.

What You Need to Succeed

The good news is I can say without a doubt that for full service funding Leo Kanell Funding is the best (www.LeoKanell.com) and will secure the best funding guaranteed with full phone, email and funding service to walk you through the entire process. For those who would rather do it themselves, no worries I have created the only comprehensive business funding formula, system and program in the country. If you haven't realized it by now, let me just say that no one is more committed, passionate or happy to see someone secure funding to realize their dream business than I am. Making money helping people is great, but when I receive emails, testimonials and hear of clients who changed their lives, their family's lives and their clients lives because they were able to launch a business and fulfill their dreams, that is truly what drives me and gives it all purpose. Know this, I will do everything possible to help you to succeed in your funding journey today and into the future!

CHAPTER 20: IMPORTANT: FUNDING RULES TO LIVE BY

So Peter Parker's uncle said with great power comes great responsibility. (Remember spiderman?) And since you have now secured money for your business or will soon, there are some important things that you need to be aware of. Having personally started several profitable, successful and also some not so successful businesses there are some important funding rules to live by that will help you to succeed. Do NOT skip this, this is experience talking that will help you avoid future issues.

Spend Slowly: Unless you have an expensive piece of equipment that will allow you to begin your business immediately, I have learned through painful experience that it is essential to begin spending money on credit lines slowly. Even if you acquire an unsecured term loan and especially if you secure any type of revolving funding, begin by spending slowly. Continue to test out your business model and plans and then scale up gradually.

The 10% Rule: Let's say that you have a new marketing plan and some additional projects and you estimate that they will cost $50,000, and since you secured $60,000 in unsecured credit lines, you have just enough money available. However, although this might be very profitable, you should probably start out by using only 10% of your available credit lines to test out your theories and new projects. Even if you have experience with your business and have operated the business for years, often new projects, in particular marketing and other capital intensive projects can be highly unpredictable. So if possible begin by spending $5,000 on your new marketing and other projects, not the full $50,000, then you can measure the results and most importantly the ROI on the project to justify scaling up and spending more the next month and so forth.

Term loans vs Credit Lines: While a term loan is different from a credit line, it is understandable that if you are wanting a term loan that you may have some specific uses for the money right away. Also, since a term loan is different from a credit line/card in that you will be paying interest on all of the money from day 1, it is understandable that you will probably spend the term loan money quicker. Utilizing a term loan to pay off credit card debt or other high interest loans is a good use for it, of course paying for expensive equipment and other expensive items that require a lot of cash like payroll for new staff/employees or money down to be able to lease an office or business location that your business must have is a justifiable capital outlay as well.

Prove your plan works, then scale it up gradually: So back to our example, let's say you began with $5,000 and over a month of testing the new marketing and projects you note that you have created new sales of $7,000 which means you have covered your initial costs of $5,000 and netted $2,000 in profits. Now perhaps, the next month you can begin with $10,000 or $15,000 and scale up your results. One of the most important lessons I have learned in business is it's not the smartest or the strongest that always succeed, it is those business owners who are able to adapt and pivot to make changes that truly succeed. If you begin by spending all of your available capital on credit lines then if your hypothesis is incorrect, you will have no more capital

© The Business Funding Formula 2017

in order to make changes and work out tweaks to your growth plans. So if you spend 5k that doesn't produce real results, sales and profits, you will still have 55k available to make changes in order to bring new sales and profits.

Business vs Personal financing: We have been taught since young for the most part that debt is a bad thing and from a personal standpoint that can certainly be true. If you rack up 10k in credit card debt to pay for a vacation, a big screen and furniture for your place, none of that is likely to make you any money. You literally spend 10k and there is no return on the money, no new profits or sales to pay back the 10k except your regular income.

With business debt like credit lines or term loans you can spend $10,000 and that can literally make you $20,000 in new sales that you would not have made without the money. In that sense the ability to generate new sales, profits and money from the funding that your business secures, makes business funding a smart choice. Smartly utilized financing that is used to generate new income for your business are what set business financing apart from personal financing.

Business Only: With your business credit lines and loans, it is vital that you spend the money only on business expenses that will generate new sales and profits for your business. Do not under any circumstances utilize the money for personal reasons. Business funding is not to ever be used for personal expenses. Of course certain travel, meals and other entertainment expenses can have business uses if they are truly used to land new clients and secure new sales for your company. Other than that, you should avoid using your business funding for anything personal unless of course you are paying off high interest personal credit cards or loans, that of course makes complete sense.

Keep a Buffer for Emergencies: Another very important rule that you will want to follow, is to always keep a couple of months of business expenses available. Buffers in your business checking account as well as in available credit with your unsecured credit lines/cards will provide capital for the unexpected. Expect the unexpected when it comes to starting a business. Emergencies and setbacks will occur, just plan on that happening, by having available credit and a buffer of money in your business bank account you will build some backup capital. A good rule is to just consider that the last 25% of your credit lines is not available except for emergencies or great opportunities that you are very confident in.

Spend Money Only if You are 95% sure it will make you twice as much: For example if a piece of equipment will help your business make more money and double sales in a few months then of course that makes sense. If there is any question in your mind about whether or not a business purchase will generate new sales and profits, stay patient and let it pass. Only spend money on business purchases that are highly likely to make you significant money.

Of course, I realize that in some cases you may not be entirely sure of a business purchase generating more sales, but of all of your opportunities it may seem like your best chance. No doubt, business comes with risks and isn't always an exact science. Sam Walton, who if still alive today would be the world's wealthiest man thanks in part to the funding formula, always made his team prove to him why an investment in technology or a business purchase would actually be a worthwhile buy for his business. Take that same approach to any tech purchases or investment in your business, sometimes more time will make it clear whether a new business purchase or investment will prove worthwhile or not.

SET UP AUTOMATIC PAYMENTS: With credit lines it is very important to set up automatic payments so that your credit lines, term loans and other business financing is always paid on time. Unlike personal loan payments, business loan payments must be made on time, even if they are a day late, that can have a negative impact on your business credit rating. So make sure you set up automatic payments for all business credit cards, lines and loans. Late payments will eliminate your 0% intro periods with unsecured credit lines/cards, automatic payments will assure that payments are made on time and your 0% intro rates are maintained.

God Bless
My entrepreneurial friends it has been my great honor to break down the rules of funding success and to reveal how the business funding formula can help you to accomplish one of the most rewarding experiences that exists in life, that of entrepreneurship. We only get one shot at life and to live the life of our dreams so don't waste a second, eliminate tv viewing and all of those activities that do not build your family and your business. After you secure the funding you need, go and focus the majority of your time, talents and resources towards generating sales and revenues. May God bless you and your family on this most beautiful of journeys and email me all of your experiences to

info@leokanell.com I would love to hear about your funding experiences and your results.

To find out how much funding you can qualify for, go to www.LeoKanell.com and we will tell you within 24 hours what your Custom Funding Plan might look like for free.

© The Business Funding Formula 2017

Made in the USA
Monee, IL
26 February 2024